AUTHOR

Eduardo Manuel Gil Martínez (June 25, 1970) historian and passionate about Spanish history, the Second World War and the Age of the Reconquista. Author of numerous texts on World War II for Spanish and Italian magazines such as "Revista Española de Historia Militar", AMARTE, "Ritterkreuz" or "The Axis Forces in World War II 1939-1945". In addition to the title we publish he is also the author of: "Sevilla Reina y Mora. Historia del reino independiente sevillano. Siglo XI ", "Breslau 1945. El último bastión del Reich", "The Spaniards in the SS and the Wehrmacht. 1944-45. The Ezquerra unit in the Battle of Berlin "," The Bulgarian Air Force in World War II. Germany's forgotten ally "," Romanian Armored Forces in World War II "," Hungarian Armored Forces in World War II "," Spanish Air Force in World War II "," Hispano Aviación Ha-1112" (about the last Messerschmitt 109 ever built in Spain) and other texts for important publishers such as Almena, Kagero, Schiffer and Pen & Sword.

PUBLISHING'S NOTES

None of unpublished images or text of our book may be reproduced in any format without the expressed written permission of Luca Cristini Editore (already Soldiershop.com) when not indicate as marked with license creative commons 3.0 or 4.0. Luca Cristini Editore has made every reasonable effort to locate, contact and acknowledge rights holders and to correctly apply terms and conditions to Content.

Every effort has been made to trace the copyright of all the photographs. If there are unintentional omissions, please contact the publisher in writing at: info@soldiershop.com, who will correct all subsequent editions.

Our trademark: Luca Cristini Editore@, and the names of our series & brand: Soldiershop, Witness to war, Museum book, Bookmoon, Soldiers&Weapons, Battlefield, War in colour, Historical Biographies, Darwin's view, Fabula, Altrastoria, Italia Storica Ebook, Witness To History, Soldiers, Weapons & Uniforms, Storia etc. are herein @ by Luca Cristini Editore.

Soldiershop is not responsible for the opinions expressed by its authors and collaborators in the context of the books we publish.

ACKNOWLEDGEMENTS

Special thanks go to Massimiliano Afiero for his help with most of the iconography. The rest of the images are mostly from American, Russian, German and British national archives for free use.

LICENSES COMMONS

This book may utilize part of material marked with license creative commons 3.0 or 4.0 (CC BY 4.0), (CC BY-ND 4.0), (CC BY-SA 4.0) or (CC0 1.0). We give appropriate attribution credit and indicate if change were made in the acknowledgments field. Our WTW books series utilize only fonts licensed under the SIL Open Font License or other free use license.

For a complete list of Soldiershop titles please contact Luca Cristini Editore on our website: www.soldiershop.com or www.cristinieditore.com. E-mail: info@soldiershop.com

BAUTZEN 1945: THE LAST VICTORY OF THE TERZO REICH. Code WTW-022 EN
By Eduardo Manuel Gil Martínez. Translated from Spanish by Anna Cristini
ISBN code: 97888932727204, First edition Marzo 2021
Language: English Size: 177,8x254mm Cover & Art Design: Luca S. Cristini

WTW (SOLDIERSHOP) is a trademark of Luca Cristini Editore, via Orio, 35/4 - 24050 Zanica (BG) ITALY.

WITNESS TO WAR

BAUTZEN 1945

THE LAST VICTORY OF THE THIRD REICH

PHOTOS & IMAGES FROM WORLD WARTIME ARCHIVES

EDUARDO MANUEL GIL MARTÍNEZ

CONTENTS

Introduction .... Pag. 5

The contenders...Pag. 13

Geographical area of the battle of Bautzen................................ Pag. 31

The precedents of the battle... Pag. 33

The battle of Bautzen.. Pag. 59

End of the German offensive and retreat .... Pag. 85

Results and conclusions.. Pag. 89

Maps and charts... Pag. 96

Bibliography... Pag. 98

▲ Soldiers belonging to an armored division in 1945. The German troops, in enormous numerical inferiority of men and means, compensated in part thanks to a first-rate armament. This fact allowed him to often come out victorious in isolated or fortuitous and particular clashes like the one that took place near the Silesian town of Bautzen.

INTRODUCTION

In the historiography of the last months of the Second World War, the last three famous attacks carried out by the German troops on the western front have always been particularly highlighted: the battle of the Ardennes (between 16 December 1944 and 25 January 1945), the battle of the Hürtgen forest (between 14 September 1944 and 10 February 1945 to the east of the German-Belgian border), and that on the eastern front with the operation "Spring Awakening" (between 6 and 16 March 1945 on Hungarian land). Both in the Ardennes and in the offensive in Hungary, after an initial moment of success, the result was always unfavorable to the German Reich, facing the overwhelming enemy superiority. On the contrary, in the battle of the Hürtgen forest, after a series of violent fights in a heavily wooded territory, the German won a defensive victory that lasted several months, stopping the American offensive, even if they eventually had to retreat again in front of the Allied superiority.

However, these were not the last blows of a Germany cornered and condemned to fight until the end according to Adolf Hitler's plan. In spite of the global decomposition of the German troops on the western front and especially on the eastern front, even in 1945 they were able to sell their defeat at a high price. After the Vistula-Oder offensive of January 1945, Soviet forces had entered Eastern Prussia and their relentless advance continued in the first weeks of that year until the battle front temporarily stabilized on the line of the Oder and Neisse rivers. On January 31 the offensive of the Red Army was stopped by order of Moscow, after the important step forward made in only one month, which had overstretched the supply lines. From that moment on, the Soviets consolidated themselves by increasing the number of troops and weapons on the Oder-Neisse line in order to strike the final blow to the German Reich as soon as possible. It was clear that already in the spring of 1945 the war in Europe had been completely decided with the victory of the Allies from both east and west, yet the remnants of the once powerful German army continued their desperate struggle to stop as much as possible the dazzling advance of the Soviet troops through the territory of the Reich. The dizzying change in the situation on the Eastern Front prompted Adolf Hitler to change the names of his army groups, so that the Northern Army Group was renamed the Courland Army Group, the Central Army Group was called the Northern Army Group, and Army Group A was renamed the Central Army Group. Several German strongholds held out as natural obstacles against the Soviet advance, but with the disadvantage of being isolated behind enemy lines. The most significant example of stronghold was the battle that took place in early 1945 to defend the city of Breslau.

The city (both the civilian population and the small military garrison), despite multiple adversities, resisted for 82 days in an epic way to the fire of the Soviet air force, artillery, infantry and armored troops. Although they had no chance of being "rescued" by their compatriots, the encircled troops, who represented a danger in the Soviet rear, pushed some troop forces to try to eliminate these bastions as Breslau, and therefore could not be used for the final advance on the Reich. In this sense (and only in this sense), the result was the desired one, since many men of the triumphant Soviet army were kept away from the front line of the advance, engaged in terrible street fighting that ended only after the fall of the capital of the Reich itself. The signing and making official of Breslau's surrender took place on May 7, while, as is well known, on May 2 around 1 p.m., the resistance in Berlin "officially" ended. The tenacious resistance of Breslau's men gave rise to an absurd situation as reported by a Russian journalist: "The victorious Soviet troops were returning from Berlin for the Victory Parade in Moscow. On their way they suddenly heard explosions and gunfire. And one person asked, "Has anyone fired into the air?" receiving a laconic answer, "No, it's the Sixth Army that is still trying to take Breslau."

In the March-April 1945 period, not much could be expected from the exhausted and shattered Ger-

▲ A young grenadier belonging to the 1st Armored Parachute Division "Hermann Göring" carrying a panzerfaust 60 on his shoulder, Gewehr 41 rifle and M-24 stick grenade. In addition to the youthfulness of the soldier, we note that the helmet and clothing of the parachute unit does not differ from that used by other units of the German army. Massimiliano Afiero Archive.

man troops en route to the Reich after Operation Bagration in the east and the Normandy landings in the west, both in 1944. Although both the Western Allies and the Soviets were advancing fast on the remnants of the Reich, it was clear to all that, in the last three months of the conflict in Europe, the main resistance of the German troops, and thus most of their war potential, was willing to try to hold off the Red Army as long as possible. In spite of the Allies' immeasurable dominance of the skies and their almost infinite military power in both armor and men, German troops achieved some small victories. We are not referring to decisive victories, however they managed to momentarily stop the Soviet assault. These small delays in the Soviet advance represented for many the possibility to flee towards the West (and therefore towards the territories occupied by the American and British troops) especially thousands of civilians and soldiers who knew of the barbaric behavior of the Soviets since their entry into the territory of the Reich (the Russians had not forgotten the atrocities committed previously by the Germans in the USSR and took the opportunity for their terrible revenge).

One of these small "victories" took place in the Seelow Hills, just over 50 kilometers from Berlin. This strategic position consisted of small hills facing a plain, from where the Soviet advance was expected. The capital of the Reich was less than a hundred kilometers from the front and became the main objective of the 11 armies that formed the 1st Belorussian Front (equivalent to the Belorussian Army Group) under the command of Marshal Zhukov, who at that time was advancing on the central region of Germany in the offensive towards Seelow-Berlin.

In the early dawn hours of April 16, 1945, Zhukov's forces in conjunction with those further south corresponding to the seven armies of the 1st Ukrainian Front (First Ukrainian Group) of Marshal Koniev began the offensive, which would finally have as its objective the city of Berlin, executed simultaneously with that covering the south of Germany which had as targets Spremberg and Torgau. In particular, the 1st Ukrainian Front had to break the defense of the 4th German Panzer Army in the Neisse, defeat the remaining German forces in Lusatia (the easternmost region of Saxony), reach the Elbe, take Dresden and Wittenberg, and complete the encirclement that was closing in on Berlin, isolating the capital from the rest of the German troops still in fighting order in southern Germany and Czechoslovakia. Finally, the 1st Ukrainian Front also had to establish contact with American troops, preventing them from crossing the Elbe River. At the same time as the previous fronts (1st Belorussian Front and 1st Ukrainian Front), further north, the 2nd Belorussian Front launched the Stettin-Rostock offensive, and the 1st Ukrainian Front the Cottbus-Postdam offensive; both were framed within the offensive launched from the Oder-Neisse line.

On the other side of the Oder-Neisse line were the German defenses, which could count 400,000 men eagerly awaiting for the attack. These defensive forces were led by General Heinrici (commanding the Vistula Army Group, which included the German Ninth Army and Third Panzer Army) and Field Marshal Schörner (with the Central Army Group, which included the Fourth Panzer Army). The ratio of men to equipment was clearly in favor of the attackers. In men the ratio was 5 to 1, 15 to 1 in guns, 5 to 1 in tanks, and 3 to 1 in aviation.

When Zhukov began his offensive, moving his 750,000 men and 1,800 tanks, he headed to the western bank of the Oder River to the so-called Küstrin bridgehead. There, his command post would be installed to begin the offensive that would reach Berlin by the shortest route, represented by the Küstrin-Berlin road. In front of their positions was the town of Seelow and the hills that were named after the town. These extended for about 45 kilometers, constituting the strong point of the German defense system in that area, which was about 145 kilometers long.

At 5 a.m., Zhukov gave the signal to fire the rockets that would start the artillery bombardment. Some 17,000 field guns, mortars and katyushas launched a terrible fire that could be heard even in the eastern part of Berlin.

The shelling continued for half an hour, pounding trenches, literally destroying the heights of Seelow.

At 5:30 a.m. the Eighth Army and the Third and Fifth Assault Armies advanced toward Seelow Heights, confident that after the great artillery barrage they received, the remaining defenses would be all but "swallowed up by the earth." Moreover, to make the action of the defenses that survived the barrage more difficult, 140 powerful anti-aircraft lights were used to dazzle them and to facilitate the passage of their troops.

These proved to be of little use, as the dust and smoke only contributed to worsening the visibility of the Soviet advance zone.

Eventually, the first infantry units reached the first German defense lines, where they quickly sensed that the Germans were all but wiped out, which, coupled with the lack of German artillery response, made them suspicious of the true state of the defenders.

Regardless, the Soviets continued to advance, marching their tanks along the roads and avoiding the swampy plains.

Crouching along Seelow Heights, the Germans waited patiently after evacuating the first line of defense before the enemy artillery bombardment;

▲ Teenager in a Volksturm battalion. Many Volksturm men and Hitler Youth boys served in the Bautzen garrison, bravely facing the enemy troops. Massimiliano Afiero Archive.

this was the cause of the virtual absence of significant casualties despite the virulence of that bombardment. The line of defense where the Germans were now arranged corresponded to about 55 kilometers from the center of the eastern defense system, which was defended by the most powerful of the three German armies, General Busse's Ninth Army. Nevertheless, their actual state was much weaker than their theoretical one and they would have to work some miracles if they wanted to stop the Soviets. Among the defensive lines was the 9th Parachute Division, once an elite unit, but now becoming a second-rate unit composed of Luftwaffe men. Although the paratroopers were not initially on the front lines, the tactical withdrawal of their comrades left them as the first German front in the area on the way to Chuikov's 67th Division.

When the armored units entered the range of the German artillery, they began to fire causing significant damage to Soviet tanks and vehicles.

At the same time, the 9th Parachute Division opened fire, passing over the Russian infantry that was in front of their positions and the armored units that had managed to escape the German artillery; as a result of the German tactics, the Soviet advance, a priori thought to be a military cakewalk for Zhukov, was completely halted. In any case, the few German forces decreased in numbers because of the heavy losses suffered during this defense of the hills.

As we have said, Marshal Koniev began his earlier bombardment on a front extending 39 kilometers south from the union of the Neisse and the Oder. Using seven armies with a total of about 500,000 men and 1,400 tanks, he planned a double assault. The first, led by the Fifth Defense Army and the

Thirteenth Army, with the Third and Fourth Armored Defense Armies in tow, would head for the Elbe and support Zhukov from south of Berlin. The second assault, with the Fifty-Second Army and the Second Polish Army, would head for Dresden.

To confuse the Germans on their main line of attack, Koniev ordered his air force and artillery to create a dense screen of smoke along the entire length of the Neisse Valley.

After 40 minutes of bombardment, prefabricated assault bridges were installed on the other side and the Soviet assault began on the "stunned" German defenses of the Fourth Panzer Army. In several areas they were overwhelmed, although a few pockets of resistance remained that resisted the initial Soviet push, which did not prevent Koniev's outposts from approaching Spremberg about 120 kilometers southeast of Berlin.

The Soviet high command was not at all happy with what had happened, because it was unexpected at this point in the war. In his haste to reach Berlin (remember that Koniev had an almost entirely free passage from the south), Zhukov forgot about the official strategies and at 2 p.m. on April 16 he sent his two tank armies along roads already full of vehicles and the remains of the Eighth Defense Army on the left and the Fifth and Third Assault Armies in the center and on the right.

The two armored armies advanced in utter confusion. That part of the Oder Valley facing the Seelow Hills soon became a succession of jammed vehicles and soldiers going from one side to the other. Only the leading military units were beyond the huge jams and able to fight, and under those circumstances the Germans were able to contain them.

By nightfall, the 9th Parachute Division was about to be overrun. After their first action, the young soldiers retreated into the hills, repelling one attack after another. That same night, Zhukov held a radio conversation with Stalin that prompted Zhukov to head north to attack with Koniev's armored armies in Berlin.

▲ German gunner at his defensive position on the Oder-Neisse front. In many sections the Neisee River was not a real obstacle for the Soviets, as this river in some areas was only 15 m wide with a depth of no more than 1 m. Massimiliano Afiero Archive.

Thus began the second day of battle on the Seelow Heights on April 17. German weakness was beginning to show, and the Soviet forces seemed never-ending. Even an army held in reserve until then (the 47th) was sent into combat. This continued attrition required the urgent dispatch of the German reserves of the 56th Panzer Corps to maintain the front line.

Koniev's important progress and Zhukov's slowdown pushed Stalin to change Koniev's orders, authorizing him to head to Berlin from the south. This degenerated into a race between the two Soviet marshals to be the first to take Berlin.

On April 18, when Koniev began his advance into the German capital, Zhukov was still "stuck" on the heights of Seelow. Eventually, his armored vehicles were able to advance about 15-20 kilometers southwest of Seelow and west of Wriezen, but without being able to break through the German defense.

April 19 saw the German defenses collapse as Zhukov's men finally opened the desired breach. Both the Eighth Defense Army and Chuikov's First Armored Army made their way to Müncheberg, about 30 kilometers east of the outskirts of Berlin. The fate of Berlin was now sealed.

This combat in Seelow Heights was an example of the only action German troops could do at this stage of the war, delay the Soviet advance, in this case for only three days. Yes, only three days, but this time on the one hand allowed for the escape to the west of civilians whose localities had already been occupied by the Russians or were about to be occupied; on the other hand it allowed the troops stationed in Berlin to improve their defenses as much as possible for what was coming.

The exact losses suffered by both armies in the Seelow Hills are not known, but probably at least 30,000 Russian soldiers died while on the German side there were about 11,000 deaths of the 18,000 men defending the lower hills, leaving the Third Panzer Army decimated by about 80,000 soldiers in a week of fighting.

In the two cases mentioned, Breslau and Seelow, the German troops managed to resist the Soviets to a greater or lesser extent, causing them a great number of human and material losses and above all managing to slow down the inexorable advance of the Red Army. But there was one last battle in which the remnants of several German units managed to articulate an attack against the advance of the Polish-Soviet troops; not only did they stop the advance, but they achieved an important tactical victory causing a large number of enemy losses in men and material. Although it may seem impossible, this combat, which was called the Battle of Bautzen, took place between April 22 and 26, 1945, when the capital of the Reich, already surrounded, faced its tragic fate. This battle was not limited to the city itself, but extended over dozens of kilometers of rural areas along the Niesky-Bautzen line, especially in the northeast and northwest.

We cannot forget that already on April 21, the 2nd Armored Guard Corps had approached Berlin from the northeast and advanced toward it, occupying the territory between the Weissensee (occupied by the 1st Mechanized Corps) and the vicinity of Hohenschönhausen (occupied by the 12th Armored Guard). Between them, troops of the 3rd and 5th assault armies were mixed at each end.

From the Rüdersdorf-Erkner area, troops of the 8th Guard Army and the 1st Guard Armored Army, which also advanced toward the Reich capital, carried out an encirclement maneuver to the southwest, with the aim of approaching the city both from the south and from the area located to the southeast.

The 3rd Armored Army of the Guard reached Königs Wusterhausen, completing the siege of the 9th German Army south of the German capital. The last hope of liberating Berlin from the siege, represented by the German 9th Army, had been shattered.

The Soviet offensive of April 16 was conducted along the entire length of the Oder and Neisse rivers, and the main target was Berlin. To encourage the capture of Berlin on the southern side as well, the 1st Ukrainian Front was sent to support the attack on the city. The mission of Marshal Koniev in command of the 1st Ukrainian Front was even more complicated than that of his comrade Zhukov in command of the 1st Belorussian Front, since he had to cover a greater distance with the risk of receiving a counterattack from the 4th Panzer Army which was south of the Red Army's line of advance or from the German 9th Army which was southeast of Berlin. The main mission of the 1st Ukrainian Front units deployed further south, the Soviet 52nd Army and the Polish 2nd Army, was to head for Dresden to try to advance as far as possible before meeting their American "Allies", protecting the southern area from the 1st Ukrainian Front's armored attack on Berlin. This offensive movement was called Operation Spremberg-Torgau. But the Germans had not said their last word on this front in the southeast of the Reich.

Thus, while Berlin gradually fell into the hands of its enemies, in Saxony some experienced mechanized (panzer grenadier) and armored (Panzer) units fought with the energy of desperation against the Red Army troops, to whom a great defeat had been inflicted with a rapid and well-executed maneuver in which practically no prisoners were taken.

Despite the general collapse of the Reich symbolized by the siege of its capital, in Bautzen as mentioned, the Germans obtained their last victory, achieving once again the same objective as Seelow or Breslau: time. In this text we will recount the events that took place in that southern German city and we can see how the fighting spirit was maintained until the end thanks to the possibility of stopping the Soviets, even if only for a few hours in their overwhelming advance, allowing the evacuation of thousands of Germans to the west.

We must clarify that the fighting that took place before, during and after the battle of Bautzen in this area of Saxony was simultaneous in various points of the front. In order to try to make them more

▲ Image of the remains of the city of Dresden after heavy bombardment by the Western Allies. However, for the Poles and Soviets covering the southern flank of the 1st Ukrainian Front it represented their main target. Bundesarchiv, Bild 183Z0309310 G. Beyer CC-BY-SA 3.0

comprehensible to the reader, we have divided the fighting into two parts on each of the days on which these lasted as a whole: one part is devoted to the events which took place in the town of Bautzen with the fighting for its capture by the Soviets and the subsequent German reconquest, and the other part is devoted to all the troop movements with their corresponding attacks, counterattacks, sieges, etc., which took place both in the east and in the west. The other part is dedicated to all troop movements with their corresponding attacks, counterattacks, sieges, etc., which took place both east and west of this city and which are framed within the fighting aimed at the capture of the Saxon capital of Dresden. And to finish the clarification, although the Battle of Bautzen itself took place between April 21 and 26, 1945, this action would not be understandable at all if it were not connected to the advance of Polish and Soviet troops through eastern Saxony and the various actions that the Germans took after reorganizing themselves in the face of the great assault of the Red Army that occurred when they crossed the German defensive line located on the Oder and Neisse rivers.

As a preliminary note to the text that follows, we must clarify that, in order to facilitate the understanding of the names of the different German, Soviet and Polish units, they have generally been translated in English. In some cases we have decided to write both the English name and the German original, if that would be more useful to some readers. Only in a few cases has the German nomenclature been retained because of its difficult translation or because it was considered more appropriate, as in the case of the Volksturm or Volksgrenadier or Panzer divisions (except in the case of the Hermann Göring 1 Parachute Division, where we preferred to use the term armored armies rather than Panzer). The same happens in the case of the different ranks, which in most cases have been written in English, leaving them in the original German when considered more appropriate to facilitate understanding. In the case of the names of the various populations that appear throughout the text, they have generally been kept in their original language because they usually have no specific known equivalent in English.

▲ Iván Stepánovich Koniev photographed while inspecting an infantry unit.

THE CONTENDERS

The German troops on the other side of the Neisse were none other than the remnants of German General Ferdinand Schörner's Central Army Group; specifically with the 4th Panzer Army and the 17th Army, under the command of Panzertruppen General Fritz-Hübert Gräser. This 4th Panzer Army consisted of four army corps:

- 5th Army Corps.
- Panzer-Korps "Grossdeutschland".
- LVII Panzer-Korps.
- Korpsgruppe "Moser."

This still powerful 4th Panzer Army was assigned the mission of defending the route to Dresden between Cottbus and Görlitz. The most imposing of its groupings was the Panzer-Korps "Grossdeutschland," under the command of General der panzertruppen Georg Jauer, which occupied a fairly quiet sector after the Vistula-Oder offensive and the subsequent German counterattack at Lauban (one of the last notable German victories on the Eastern Front and in the war), which made the Soviet troops somewhat calmer as they awaited the final blow against the Reich.

▲ Soldiers belonging to the 1st Armored Parachute Division "Hermann Göring" pose for the photographer on April 25, 1945 in Kubschütz, a village near Bautzen, after recapturing the town from the Soviets. Although they look tired, the photo shows the high fighting spirit of the men in this unit just days before the German capitulation. Most of these men sport various types of weapons such as the Gewehr 43, the Mauser 98k or the Soviet Mosin Nagant equipped with telescopic sights. The soldier on the left of the photo continues to wear a paratrooper helmet, as opposed to the classic helmet worn by his unit despite the fact that it is "in theory" made up of paratroopers. Archived by Massimiliano Afiero.

▲ Men belonging to the command of the 1st Parachute Armored Division "Hermann Göring" inspect a destroyed Soviet position near Kleinwelka, near Bautzen. A Steyr ambulance stands in the background and the vehicle behind them, an Opel Kadett convertible with the emblem of Panzer-Korps "Hermann Göring". Afiero Archive.

▼ Famous photograph showing two Panther Ausf G tanks of the 1st Parachute Armored Division "Hermann Göring" marching along a road through a forest during the days of the Battle of Bautzen. The armored vehicles are accompanied on either side of the road by grenadiers belonging to the 2nd Regiment of the 1st Armored Parachute Division "Hermann Göring". The soldier on the left of the photo is still wearing the helmet typical of parachute units. The photo is dated April 20, 1945 near Kodersdorf. Afiero Archive.

In fact, the Germans had prepared for the anticipated Soviet offensive during the three months of calm by strengthening their defenses on the banks of the Neisse and Weisse Schöps. Despite German intentions, it was clear that the troops of the 4th Panzer Army were insufficient to cover both the Neisse line and the entire route to Dresden in depth. To this end, the German High Command came to the conclusion of how difficult it would be to defend the entire length of the Neisse River against the Soviets, and so an attempt was made to halt the Soviet advance toward the Saxon capital through a series of fortified villages on the road to Dresden, which would allow the enemy's advance to be slowed and, more importantly, buy time for the mechanized and armored divisions of the 4th Panzer Army to make a decisive counterattack. The most important towns on the road to Dresden were Weissenberg and Bautzen. The first of the villages was too small to think of stopping the Red Army advance for long, but Bautzen seemed the ideal place to hold out as long as possible. The persistence of Bautzen in German hands during the Soviet advance also added another advantage for the German troops, as Bautzen was to serve as an anchor point for any counterattacks to regain lost territory. Among the units that made up these two groupings were the 20th Panzer Division, the 21st Panzer Division, the 1st Armored Parachute Division "Hermann Göring" or Fallschirm-Panzer-Division 1 "Hermann Göring" (belonging to the Panzer-Korps "Hermann Göring" which was created in 1944 when the 2nd Parachute Grenadier Division joined the 1st Armored Parachute Division "Hermann Göring"), the Panzergrenadier-Division "Brandenburg", as well as some pieces of the 17th, 62nd and 615th Infantry Division z. b.V. or the 545th Volksgrenadier Division. In addition, some other units participated to a lesser extent in the fighting, such as the supply train of the 10th SS Panzer Division "Frundsberg", the Volksturm and the Hitler Youth.

Although it is difficult to know exactly, according to various sources it has been established that the Germans of the 4th Panzer Army had about 50,000 men available to face the Soviets and the Poles (whose presence was unknown at the beginning of the fighting). As main combat equipment, they had about 600 artillery pieces, 450 armored vehicles and three hundred tanks and assault wagons (mainly Pz V "Panther" and Pz IV as well as StuG III, StuG IV, Jagdpanzer IV (of the IV L/48 model at least) and Jagdpanzer 38 "Hetzer" mainly in the armored and mechanized divisions). A favorable fact for the Germans was that although the various German armored and mechanized units were worn out, they were all first-rate, unlike the infantry units of the 4th Panzer Army. Apparently on paper it looked like a powerful grouping, but all German units had been "pushed back" for many months, and with less than a month to go before the end of the war in Europe, these units were nearly all decimated, exhausted, and extremely short of fuel and armaments; although they would still sell their defeat dearly in the days to come. We will give a brief description of the operational status of the main units engaged in the defense of the Neisse and later in the battle of Bautzen.

The deployment of the German units of the 4th Panzer Army awaiting the crossing of the Neisse was as follows: to the north, at Cottbus, was the 21st Panzer Division (which would eventually take part in the fighting for Bautzen only to the extent that this unit was originally intended to avoid encirclement of the German capital), then already facing the town of Spremberg, the defensive line was maintained by the 545th Volksgranader Division (this infantry formation was of great fighting value since it incorporated in its ranks the remnants of an elite division the 78th Sturm-Division). A little further south, between Weisswasser and Rietschen, the 615th Z.B.V. Division was deployed, short for zur besorenden Verwendung or in English "for special purposes" (which was nothing more than a group of troops put together at the last minute, where there were, among others, administrative and bureaucratic personnel who had been mobilized in view of the urgency of the situation).

As of March 1, 1945, the organization chart of the 615th Division z.b.V. was as follows:

- General Staff.
- 687th Brigade Geniery.

- 3093rd Fortress Machine Gun Battalion (festung).
- 3094th Fortress Machine Gun Battalion.
- 3095th Fortress Machine Gun Battalion.
- 1485th Fortress Infantry Battalion
- 500th Fortress Battalion.

Continuing the line of defense, the Brandenburg Division was deployed next to Rothenburg under the command of Major General Hermann Schulte-Heuthaus. This excellent unit was composed of veteran troops, many of whom belonged to the Brandenburgers, truly elite German troops. On April 1, the "Brandenburg" had 10,375 men, 2 command tanks, 2 artillery observation vehicles, 80 different types of panzers, and 3 heavy anti-tank guns.

On March 1, 1945, the organization chart of the Panzergrenadier Division "Brandenburg" was as follows:
- General Staff
- 1st Hunter Regiment (motorized) (with 1st and 2nd Battalions)
- 2nd Hunter Regiment (motorized) (with 1st and 2nd Battalions)
- Armored regiment (with 1st and 2nd battalions)
- Artillery regiment (with 1st, 2nd, and 3rd battalions)
- Artillery Battalion
- Anti-aircraft artillery battalion
- Armored Reconnaissance Battalion
- Battalion of armored assault engineers
- Armored Signal Battalion
- Replacement Battalion
- Supply Regiment

It is important to remember that at least the 1st Armored Battalion of the "Brandenburg" (equipped with Panther tanks) in the days of fighting for Bautzen that we will recount in the text, was a little further north than the bulk of the Division, as it was trapped in the Halbe pocket and therefore did not participate in the battle of Bautzen. Not far from here there was another elite German unit, the Hermann Göring Parachute Division 1. This unit was assigned to the Panzer-Korps "Hermann Göring" (founded in 1944) which already in April 1945, after violent clashes with the Soviets in Silesia, retreated neatly to the easternmost region of Saxony. The 1st Parachute Division "Hermann Göring" was left on the defensive line of Neisse. Although in a more marginal role during the fighting that we report in this text, we must mention Parachute Division 2 "Hermann Göring", also belonging on paper to the Luftwaffe. This unit was formed in September 1944 and formed the Panzer-Korps "Hermann Göring" together with its "sister" Parachute Division 1 "Hermann Göring". It was evacuated from the Baltic area near Dresden (in the north) out of the front line, and restructured within the OKH reserve. It was not until the end of April 1945 that it became operational again as part of the 4th Panzer Army of Schörner's Central Army Group, although at that time it had only 4,300 men and 15 machine guns.

As of March 1, 1945, the organization chart of Parachute Division 1 "Hermann Göring" was as follows:
- General Staff
- 1st Regiment (with 1st and 2nd Battalions)
- 2nd Regiment (with 1st and 2nd Battalions)

▲ Panther IV tank of the last model belonging to the Armored Parachute Division 1 "Hermann Göring". The photograph was taken near Hochkirch on April 23, 1945. Even in the last days of the world conflict in Europe, the German armored forces represented a great danger to their rivals. Unknown origin.

▼ Men of the 1st Armored Parachute Division "Hermann Göring" inspect the battlefield after the fighting at Kleinwelka. A Soviet ISU-122 tank destroyer, loaned by the Soviet Army to the Polish 2nd Army and belonging to the 1st Armored Division, can be seen next to the destroyed houses. On the side of the powerful armored vehicle armed with a 122 mm cannon, the symbol of the Polish white eagle can be seen. The photograph is dated April 26, 1945. Courtesy of Massimiliano Afiero.

▲ Troops of the 1st Parachute Armored Division "Hermann Göring" inspect an IS-2 heavy tank captured by the Polish 1st Armored Corps near Kleinwelka. On the side of its powerful turret armed with a 122 mm cannon, you can see the Polish white eagle symbol and the name of the tank "Tadeusz". Just to the left of the image you can also see a British or Canadian universal transport that would have arrived in the U.S.S.R. through the Lend-Lease treaties. Both vehicles fell intact into the hands of the Germans. Courtesy of Massimiliano Afiero.

▼ Elephant tank destroyer wrecked in the Bautzen area in the spring of 1945. Although this tank was at the time already obsolete to deal with its Soviet rivals, there were still some in service. Courtesy of Massimiliano Afiero.

- Armored Regiment (with 1st, 2nd and 3rd Battalions)
- Artillery Regiment (with 1st, 2nd and 3rd Battalions)
- Fusiliers Battalion
- Engineer Battalion
- Signal Battalion
- Reconnaissance Battalion
- Replacement Battalion
- Military Police Detachment
- Post Office Group
- Supply Detachment

Since its creation, the 1st Armored Parachute Division "Hermann Göring" had distinguished itself by its great combat capability and had achieved important tactical successes against the Red Army during the previous year. As of 15 April it had 12,762 men, 23 Panzer IVs (in the 2nd Battalion of the Armored Regiment), 26 Panzer V "Panther" (in the 1st Battalion of the Armored Regiment), 3 Tiger Is and five armored anti-tank vehicles. Out of curiosity, on 15 April the Division received 21 Panther tanks, originally intended for the 7th Panzer Division. The 1st Armored Parachute Division "Hermann Göring" was also characterized by its important armament endowment compared to the other divisions of the German Army; an example of this is the fact that since its creation it had an Anti-Aircraft Artillery Regiment (FlaK Regiment) instead of a Detachment

▲ Famous photograph of the front of the Panther tank belonging to the 1st Armored Battalion of the 1st Parachute Armored Division "Hermann Göring". In the command hatch we observe the battalion commander Oberstleutnant Karl Rossman who achieved important successes during the battle of Bautzen. On the side of his Panther is painted in white an insignia representing a Centaur and the serial number of the engine.

(Abteilung). Moreover, throughout the course of the conflict, this artillery regiment was equipped (in January 1945, a few months before our story) with 84 88 mm cannons, 40 3.7 cm cannons, 45 2 cm cannons and 83 vehicles equipped with anti-aircraft artillery pieces. For its part, the Panzer-Korps "Hermann Göring", in addition to bringing together the two divisions with the same name, also had its own units such as the Command Company, Artillery, Assault Troops, Press, Health, Engineers, Military Police and a few others that would have the opportunity to participate in the fighting in the days to come.

To finish with the German defensive layout in the sector between Görlitz and Lauban we find two divisions of the LVII Panzer-Korps, the 17th and 72nd Infantry Divisions. Both units had a good level of training of their troops, but they had a rather small number of soldiers. Finally, as a strong unit in the area, there was the 20th Panzer Division which had been under the command of Major General Hermann von Oppeln-Bronikowski since November 1944 (a veteran of the Battle of Kursk and Normandy and an Olympic medalist at the Berlin Olympics). This powerful unit had on April 1 13,569 men, a Panzer III, 28 Panzer IVs, 27 Panzer V "Panther", 24 Panzer IV/70s and StuGs in addition to 102 other armored units of all types.

As of March 1, 1945, the organization chart of the 20th Panzer Division was as follows:

▲ Picture of Colonel Lemke commanding the 1st Armored Parachute Division "Hermann Göring" with his adjutant during a short rest on April 8, 1945, shortly before the events described in this text. His good command skills allowed his still powerful unit to create a lot of problems for Soviet and Polish troops on the 1st Ukrainian front. Unknown origin.

▼ Several officers of the 1st Armored Parachute Division "Hermann Göring" photographed on April 20, 1945, probably in the Görlitz area On the left of the photo is a camouflaged bus with a German cross painted on it. Unknown origin.

- General Staff
- 76th Panzer Regiment (with 1st, 2nd, and 3rd battalions)
- 90th Panzer Grenadier Regiment (with 1st, 2nd, and 3rd battalions)
- 8th Armored Battalion
- 20th Artillery Regiment (with 1st, 2nd and 3rd Battalions)
- 284th Anti-Aircraft Artillery Battalion
- 285th Anti-Aircraft Artillery Battalion
- 120th Armored Reconnaissance Battalion
- 20th Anti-tank Battalion
- 20th Replacement Battalion
- 20th Armored Signal Battalion
- 20th Supply Regiment

We will also comment on the organization chart of another unit noted for its more marginal involvement in the events we will report; we refer to the General Staff of Panzer-Korps "Grossdeutschland" as of 1 March 1945:

- Heavy Armored Battalion
- Rifle Regiment (with 1st and 2nd Battalions and Regimental Support Company)
- Armored Replacement Regiment
- 44th Signal Battalion
- Personnel of the 500th Artillery Brigade (with an observation battery and the 500th Armored Artillery Regiment)
- 500th Engineer Motorized Regiment
- 500th Armored Engineer Battalion
- 500th Reconnaissance Unit (with half-tracks)
- 500th Personnel Escort Company
- 500th Sound Position Platoon (motorized)
- 500th Mapping Detachment
- 500th Military Police Detachment
- 500th Motorized Supply Regiment

The Panzer-Korps "Grossdeutschland", after its creation in September 1944, in addition to its general staff, consisted mainly of its two most powerful units, the Panzer-Grenadier Division "Grossdeutschland" and the Panzer-Grenadier Division "Brandenburg", although these would never be able to fight as a single unit on the same front. The first, in fact, did not participate in the events that we will report while the second, on the contrary, was one of the main protagonists.

It is interesting to know the organization chart of the 4th Panzer Army as of April 18, 1945, even though at that time, after the Red Army attack, the constituent units of the 4th Panzer Army had been largely disorganized along the Neisse front, and in many cases practically cut off from each other (in fact, some of the units, being in the northern part of the gap caused by the enemy, would have had no or a minimal role in the battles of Bautzen). Only the German effort and perseverance in the face of the great disaster that had occurred only a couple of days before made it possible to create again a minimally stable front line and even to be able to counterattack the Soviets and the Poles. The organizational chart was as follows:

4th Panzer Army:

a) Korps Gr Gen d'Art Moser (under the command of Artillery General Willi Morser).
- 193rd Division
- 404th Division
- 464th Division

b) V. Armeé-Korps (Army Corps) under the command of Artillery General Kurt Wägner
- 21st Panzer Division under General Heinrinch Hermann von Hülsen (on 15 April still a reserve of the Heersgruppe of the 4th Panzer Army)
- 275th Infantry Division (under Lt. Gen. Hans Schmidt)
- 342nd Infantry Division (under Lt. Gen. Heinrich Nickel)
- Kampfgruppe 36th SS Pz Grenadier Division (under SS-Oberführer Oskar Dirlewanger).
- 214th Infantry Division (under Lieutenant General Harry von Kirchbach).
- Kampfgruppe 35th SS Polizei-Grenadier Division (under SS-Standartenführer Rüdigen Pipkorn)

c) Panzer-Korps "Grossdeutschland
- 615th Division z.b.V. (under the "temporary" command of Oberst der Reserve von Below) which, as mentioned above, consisted of: 687th Army Engineer Brigade, 3093rd, 3094th and 3104th Garrison Battalions, 1485th Fort Infantry Battalion and 500th Battalion
- Kampfgruppe of the 545th Volksgrenadier Division (under the command of General Hans Ernst Kohlsdorfer)
- Führer-Begleit- FBD Division under Oberst Otto Ernst Remer (on 15 April it was still a reserve of the Heersgruppe of the 4th Panzer Army)
- 10th SS Panzer Division "Frundsberg" under SS-Brigadeführer Heinz Harmel and relieved on April 27 by Field Marshal Ferdinand Schörner to be replaced by SS-Obersturmführer Franz Roestel (on April 15 it was still in reserve for the OKH or Army High Command)
- 344th Division under Lt. Gen. Erwin Jolase

d) LVII Panzer-Korps
- 6th Volksgrenadier Division (under Lt. Gen. Otto Brücker)
- 72nd Infantry Division under Lt. Gen. Hermann Hohn (until 20 April, then Lt. Gen. Hugo Beisswänger)
- 1st Armored Parachute Division "Hermann Göring" under General Max Lemke (on 15 April still a reserve of the Heersgruppe of the 4th Panzer Army)
- 20th Panzer Division under the command of General Hermann von Oppeln-Bronikowski (on 15 April still a reserve for the OKH or Army High Command)
- Panzergrenadier Division "Brandenburg" under the command of Generalmajor Hermann Schulte-Heuthaus
- Görlitz (city defense troops)

e) Panzer-Korps "Hermann Göring" under the command of Lieutenant General Wilhelm Schmalz (on 15 April still in transit from East Prussia)

Parachute Armored Division 2 "Hermann Göring" (under the command of General Erich Walther) on April 15 was still in transit from East Prussia and as already mentioned was in a period of reorganization near Dresden.

Finally, we will make special mention of the groups that formed the fighting forces tasked with defending the town of Bautzen. Their garrison had 3,000 men belonging to two battalions of the Territorial Army, Landesschützen Bataillone 992 and 393; as well as two other units of the Volkssturm, Volkssturm-Bataillone 27/32 under the command of Major Schober and Volkssturm-Bataillone 27/33 under the command of Major Ohland. The latter two units were composed of people over the age of 60 and poorly trained teenagers under the age of 16 (the average age was 47). In most cases the weapons they had at their disposal consisted of old rifles captured from the enemy (in this case of French model) and between 5 and 25 rounds per man. Other units in the defense of the city were 45 policemen and 70 boys of the Hitler Youth.

The defenders of Bautzen also had some Italian grenades and the much needed (for anti-tank fighting) panzerfaust, as well as a few MG 34 machine guns. Each Volkssturm battalion had 600 men and was organized with one command company and three line companies. The defense of the city was supplemented by a handful of artillery pieces: a 37mm antiaircraft battery deployed on the heights of Burk, a heavy battery from Flak-Abteilung 521 (521st artillery unit) at Neupurschwitz covering the approaches to the Bautzen-Weissenberg route, another battery from Flak-Abteilung 658 protecting the southeast at Rabitz, and a final battery from Flak-Abteilung 383 at Schafberg (with 12 88mm guns).

These small-caliber artillery pieces were obviously not suitable for antitank fire, but they were useful against infantry troops and conventional vehicles. To make matters worse, most of the personnel in the various antiaircraft batteries used to fire on the enemy on the ground were not qualified troops, but rather Hitler Youth auxiliaries. Therefore, as we can well imagine, all of these German troops deployed in Bautzen would have been no match for the powerful Polish and Soviet units that would come across them. But the order to turn Bautzen into a small bastion that would attract as many enemy troops as possible made the resistance at Bautzen much stronger than the Soviets expected.

Commanding this mix of units was Oberst Dietrich Hoepke. This soldier, a former tactics teacher at the Dresden War College, had been demobilized due to a serious knee injury during the Russian campaign and had voluntarily returned to the army after the hellish bombing of Dresden. Perhaps

▲ A T-34 medium tank belonging to the 1st Armored Regiment during a parade of the 1st Infantry Division "Tadeusz Kosciuszko". This is a T-34/75, less ptente than those used by the Polish 2nd Army in the battle for Bautzen.

▲ An ISU-122 armed with a powerful 122 mm piece as it crosses the Neisse. In some areas, fording the river was even easier with only about 15 m wide and a depth of no more than 1 m. Unknown origin.

▼ An ISU-122 self-propelled gun belonging to the 25th Self-Propelled Artillery Regiment of the Polish 1st Armored Corps. The armored vehicle in the photo is crossing a bridge built for crossing the Neisse by troops of the 1st Ukrainian Front. Unknown origin.

this situation, added to the orders he received to defend Bautzen to the end, generated in Hoepke a maniacal determination towards the city. By trying to keep as many Soviet troops as possible pinned down in a thousand urban battles to prevent them from advancing further toward Dresden, he was able to buy enough time for the German armored and mechanized units to push back and regroup for a counteroffensive. In addition, the troops that would fight for Bautzen were reinforced by about 200 men belonging to the 10th SS Panzer Division "Frundsberg," whose vehicles had run out of gasoline and were left in the city when their division was sent north. The presence of these men was incidental, as Hitler had claimed the presence of this division (which was deployed southeast of Görlitz as a reserve) to support the troops in Berlin. Most of the division marched north, but when Red Army attacks occurred in Saxony, the 10th SS Panzer-Artillery Regiment and the 10th SS Panzer Aufklärungs-Abteilung remained in the Bautzen area and eventually reinforced the city.

But these were not the only men to strengthen the defense of Bautzen, as after the Soviet attack on the Niesse defensive line, several units fell under the command of Oberst Dietrich Hoepke during their retreat. We refer (according to Mahé's studies) to a disciplinary Company of the 4th Panzer Army (Bewärungs-Kompanie), the 831st Ost Battalion (composed of Volga Tatars), the 96th Sturmflak-Abteilung (belonging to the 47th Anti-Aircraft Artillery Regiment) and the survivors of a Company of the 1244th Grenadier Regiment (I./Grenadier-Regiment 1244). In addition, perhaps on 19 April, two units of little military value, although suitable for defensive combat, were incorporated into the defenses of Bautzen, as were the 1459th and 1461st Fortress Infantry Battalions (Festungs-Infanterie-Bataillonen) that had withdrawn from Görlitz. More powerful than the Volksturm were the fortress infantry battalions, which numbered 695 men and had 12 heavy machine guns, 36 light machine guns, 54 panzerchreck, 70 panzerfaust and 12.8 cm mortars.

Despite its "ancient" status as a fortress, the city of Bautzen had virtually no modern fortifications. The city was located on a plateau looking toward the Spree River, and at the top of this plateau was

▲ Remains of buildings in Bautzen in 1945. The fighting that took place in the city during both the Soviet attack and the German counterattack left most of the city's buildings reduced to rubble. Unknown origin.

▲ Remains of a Jagdanzer IV after being attacked by Soviet artillery in Hungary. The Panzer-Grenadier Division "Brandenburg" had a unit equipped with these tank destroyers that were still very effective against the enemy. Unknown origin.

▶ Photograph of the most decorated German soldier of World War II, Hans Ulrich Rudel, who with his Stukas with two 37mm cannons caused terror to Soviet and Polish armored vehicles during the Battle of Bautzen. He was the only German military officer to receive the highest decoration awarded in Germany of the Third Reich, the Iron Cross with Oak Leaves in gold, swords and diamonds.

▼ A Polish IS-2, as seen by the men riding it, advances through German territory. Once the German defensive lines at the Neisse River were broken after the April 16, 1945 attack, the magnificent German road network aided the rapid advance of enemy armored vehicles.

Ortenburg Castle surrounded by medieval walls. On the southern outskirts of the city was the train station, and to the northwest of it was König Albert's military training base.

As early as February 15, prisoners of war and forced laborers began to create defensive structures, trenches, and other elements, both in and around the city. In fact, several concentric bands of fortifications were created by taking advantage of the defensive features offered by the terrain (especially those near the Spree River), which was dotted with small defensive structures. Bautzen's command post was located in Ortenburg Castle, right on top of a hill. As a curiosity, most of the city's ancient defensive positions and fortifications faced west using the river and the city's heights as natural defenses, but as Hamilton well reflected in his work, this time the enemy came from the east.

On the Red Army side, the protagonists were the units of the 1st Ukrainian Front commanded by Marshal Koniev: the 5th Guard Army and some units of the 52nd Army, both led by General Ivan Petrov. In addition, as part of the "forced" cooperation of the Poles with their Soviet "liberators," the Second Polish Army under the command of General Świerczewski also participated in the fighting within the 1st Ukrainian Front. The 52nd Army of General K. A. Koroteiev was a powerful formation that had achieved remarkable successes during the Red Army offensive since 1943 and was already a veteran of many battles such as Korsun, Iasi-Chisinev or the recent battles in Silesia. It was therefore a very solid army that would face the southern flank of the Panzer-Korps "Grossdeutschland".

As we will see later, it was well equipped and initially consisted of:

- 7th Guard Mechanized Corps (under the command of Lieutenant General Korchagin) which included the 24th Guard Mechanized Brigade (with its main unit the 13th Guard Armored Regiment), the 25th Guard Mechanized Brigade (with its main unit the 12th Guard Armored Regiment), the 26th Guard Mechanized Brigade (with its main unit the 215th Armored Regiment), the 57th Guard Armored Brigade (consisting of 3 armored battalions), the 355th Guard Heavy Self-Propelled Artillery Regiment, the 291st Guard Self-Propelled Artillery Regiment, and the 1820th Guard Self-Propelled Artillery Regiment
- 48th Rifle Corps: which included the 116th and 294th Rifle Divisions
- 73rd Rifle Corps: which included the 50th, 111th and 254th Rifle Corps
- 78th Rifle Corps: comprising the 31st, 214th and 373rd Rifle Divisions
- 213th Rifle Division
- 214th Armored Regiment

As we can see the "spearhead" and therefore the most powerful unit of General Koroteiev's 52nd Army was evidently the 7th Guard Mechanized Corps under the command of General Korchagine, with the 57th, 24th, 25th and 26th Guard Mechanized Brigades. The other unit used on the southern flank of the 1st Ukrainian Front was the aforementioned Polish 2nd Army (Ludowe Wojsko Polskie or LWP) which on the line of attack faced the center of the Panzer-Korps "Grossdeutschland"; according to Yann Mahé's study, the Polish forces were constituted on 15 April 1945 by:

- 1st Armored Corps. 10,700 men. With 21 SU-76m, 21 SU-85, 21 ISU-152 and 210 T-34/85 and IS-2. 12 ZIS-3 76mm guns. This unit consisted of: 2nd, 3rd and 4th Armored Brigades, 1st Motorized Rifle Brigade, 24th, 25th and 27th Self-Propelled Artillery Regiments and 2nd Motorcycle Battalion.
- 5th Infantry Division. 9,909 men. 21 SU-76m. 24 ZIS-3 76mm guns. 12 howitzers of 122 and 152 mm. This unit consisted of: 13th, 15th and 17th Infantry Regiments and 22nd Light Artillery Regiment.
- 7th Infantry Division. 8,200 men. 21 SU-76m. 24 ZIS-3 76mm guns. 12 howitzers of 122 and 152 mm. This unit consisted of: 33rd, 35th and 37th Infantry Regiments and 38th Light Artillery Regiment.
- 8th Infantry Division. 9,695 men. 21 SU-76m. 24 ZIS-3 76mm guns. 12 howitzers of 122 and 152 mm. This unit consisted of: 32nd, 34th and 36th Infantry Regiments and 37th Light Artillery Regiment.

▲ A lone Panther tank driving through a German city at the end of the war. The large deployment of Soviet aircraft over the capital of the Reich left it partially unmanned in Saxony, allowing the movement of German armored troops with some impunity.

- 9th Infantry Division. 10,017 men. 21 SU-76m. 24 ZIS-3 76mm guns. 12 howitzers of 122 and 152 mm. This unit consisted of: 26th, 28th and 30th Infantry Regiments and 40th Light Artillery Regiment.
- Tenth Infantry Division. 10,475 men. 21 SU-76m. 36 ZIS-3 76mm guns. 12 howitzers of 122 and 152 mm. This unit consisted of: the 25th, 27th, and 29th Infantry Regiments and the 39th Light Artillery Regiment.
- Second Artillery Division. 5,656 men. 72 76 mm ZIS-3 cannons. 96 howitzers of 122 and 152 mm.

Other smaller support units such as the 3rd Anti-Aircraft Artillery Division, the 26th Anti-Aircraft Artillery Regiment, and the 2nd Mortar Regiment.

The power of their formation lay in the 84,000 men, supported by more than 200 tanks (including the latest evolution of the T-34 and the IS-1: the T-34/85 and the IS-2) and more than 100 self-propelled fighters (such as the SU-85 or the ISU-152). The number of Soviet troops reached 20,000.

The Polish 2nd Army initially (in January 1945) was to be used in the rear of the front to combat anti-communist underground and at the same time to demonstrate the strength of the new Soviet authorities. When they were deployed in the Polish Lublin area, it turned out that the "new" Polish army was not treated by the population as "their own", but as an army of occupation. But soon after, the Soviet high command thought it appropriate for the Polish unit to participate in the fighting on the front to cover most of the troops of the 1st Ukrainian Front in their advance toward southern Berlin; thus, from April 11, 1945 it was deployed in the drop zone of the Soviet troops who were to go to Dresden.

However, when the attack on the defensive line of Neisse began, this Polish unit was occupied with perhaps the most thankless tasks of the attack in the direction of Dresden (from which it was separated by about a hundred kilometers) as it had to open a breach in the German front and "clear" the road on the Weissenberg-Bautzen axis for the 7th Mechanized Corps of the Soviet Guard. Thus the Poles would act as battering rams and flank protectors for Korchagine's Soviet unit, which would eventually take credit for the capture of Dresden, while the Poles of the Second Polish Army would be excluded from such a victory.

At first glance, both in terms of men and equipment, these numbers could be considered very satisfactory, but in reality they were not so positive because the quality of Polish troops was not excellent. The system of enlistment in the unit was catastrophic because most of the soldiers in the Second Army were men from the Polish territories "liberated" from the Soviet army and had received only hasty military training, without any previous combat experience, and poorly educated. Since the number of men needed to activate the Polish unit had not been completed with these, Soviet citizens were sought preferably of Polish origin. Remember that after the Katyn massacre and the war years, the most experienced Polish troops hardly existed. Moreover, these recruitment problems were reflected not only in the troop, but also in the number of officers that corresponded to the formation of the unit in a ratio of 1 officer for every 1,200 troop men. Many of the officers had been "pulled" from the Soviet Army when they demonstrated some sort of ancestral relationship with Poland (called the "Polish Assignment"). About 56% of the officers were Soviet delegate officers who held most of the high-ranking command positions in the Polish Second Army, while the Polish officers (usually of lower rank) in many cases lacked any combat experience. Morale in the Polish unit was never high, despite its good armament and supplies. In fact, a good example was the mass desertion of 636 soldiers (including 2 officers) of the 31st Infantry Regiment of the 7th Infantry Division, which took place between October 12 and 13, 1944. As a result of this outrage, the 31st Infantry Regiment was disbanded.

To clarify who commanded the Polish unit, it should be mentioned that most of its commanders were Soviets of Polish origin, who were obviously disliked by the troops. To make matters worse, the unit was led by General Karol Świerczewski born in Warsaw in 1897, who had a rather dubious background, being a staunch communist. His resume began in 1915 when he served at the front in the Russian army to declare himself a communist after the 1917 revolution and join the newly formed Red Army participating in the Revolution and subsequent civil war in Russia. He then participated in the war against Poland in 1919-1920 to hold various positions within the Red Army, including that of intelligence officer. In 1936 he was sent to Spain where he fought on the side of the Republicans. During this period of participation in the Spanish Civil War served as a political commissar sent by the Soviets where he received the pseudonym of General "Walter" (nickname received for his "expertise" in the use of the Walther PP gun of German manufacture against prisoners of war and deserters) participating in many internal purges of the International Brigades. In the Spanish Civil War he also participated in the capture of Belchite, the Battle of Teruel and the Battle of Alcañiz. He was arrested during the Stalinist purges, but released and rehabilitated in 1940 (which confirmed his high position in the NKVD and his more than likely testimony against other suspects of the Stalinist regime).

During World War II he had worked for the Soviet NKVD in 1941 and participated in the defense of the USSR against German troops during Operation "Barbarossa" in the 248th Rifle Division (which was completely destroyed during the Battle of Moscow in November 1941) and in the Battle of Viazma. In all of these campaigns he never proved to be a good tactician (he is considered by modern historians as completely lacking in command skills, despite having graduated from several Soviet military schools) and in conjunction with his pro-Soviet background, he was not well liked by his native troops. Add to this his inordinate predilection for alcohol (many historians remember him as a chronic alcoholic), which led him in too many situations to decide actions and give orders to his troops while completely drunk.

From 1943 General Świerczewski was assigned by Stalin to the Polish army that was being formed in the Soviet-controlled USSR. In December 1944 he became commander of the Polish 2nd Army, despite his total lack of competence. Not only was the general viewed with contempt by his men, but the deputy head of the Polish People's Army himself, General Zygmunt Berling, came into conflict with him on numerous occasions (mainly due to his alcoholism and the obvious contempt he felt for the lives of his own soldiers), objecting to handing him the command of any unit of the Polish People's Army, but Stalin made it clear that he was the only one making decisions in the Red Army and decided otherwise, so he kept him in command of the 2nd Polish Army. The last Soviet army to take part in the attack across the Neisse was the 5th Guard Army (under the command of General A. S. Zhadov). This unit was facing the northern flank of the Panzer-Korps "Grossdeutschland" and thus was not much involved in the events we will report. We also present their order of battle:

- 32nd Guard Rifle Corps (composed of the 13th, 95th and 97th Guard Rifle Divisions and the 9th Guard Airborne Division)
- 33rd Guard Rifle Corps (composed of the 14th and 78th Guard Rifle Divisions and the 118th Guard Rifle Division)
- 34th Guards Fusilier Corps (composed of the 15th and 58th Guards Fusilier Divisions)
- 4th Guard Armored Corps (composed of the 12th, 13th and 14th Guard Armored Brigades, 3rd Guard Mechanized Rifle Brigade, 29th Guard Armored Regiment, 1660th Light Artillery Regiment, 293rd Guard Self-Propelled Artillery Regiment, plus other smaller units)
- 150th Armored Brigade.
- 39th and 226th Independent Armored Regiments.
- 1889th Self-Propelled Artillery Regiment.

Overall, and regardless of the number or name of the various German or Soviet-Polish units, the balance was clearly tilted toward the attacking side. German troops were outnumbered, ill-equipped, through great hardship, or even without supplies of food, fuel, and ammunition. Yet, at this stage of the world conflict, the matter in which the Poles did not surpass the Germans was experience, despite the existence on the German side of troops with lesser combat value, such as the Volksturm or the Hitler Youth, but who were skillfully integrated into the structures of the older units, thus increasing their combat value.

GEOGRAPHICAL AREA OF THE BATTLE OF BAUTZEN

A brief consideration on the terrain characteristics of East Saxony, also known as Lusatia (although this region now includes areas southwest of Brandenburg and southwest of Polish Silesia), is deemed necessary, as the area in which the fighting narrated in this text took place clearly marked the course of events.

Eastern Saxony had a homogeneous landscape consisting of small towns with tightly clustered buildings separated from each other by extensive agricultural fields with small hills dotted with some forests. In addition, the existence of Highway 6 and several smaller roads that connected the entire region facilitated communication not only on the east-west axis but also north-south. It is evident that the characteristics of the terrain were very favorable to the advancement of the armored formations, which could count above all on the Reich's good system of roads. On the other hand, this was also an ideal terrain for direct attack against them or through the use of air attacks; the various German attacks with ground troops and their Stukas against the advance, at times carefree, of the Poles and Soviets in what they considered a war practically over are proof of this.

After crossing the Neisse River, which was a relatively easy matter for the mighty Red Army, only the Spree River that washed Bautzen could be considered a small defensive element for the German troops. In fact, during the fighting for Bautzen, garrison commander Hoepke ordered the destruction of several bridges to try to stop the enemy's advance.

Among the most important locations on the route of Highway 6 between Dresden and Görlitz were the two towns where perhaps the bloodiest clashes for their possession occurred: Weissenberg and Bautzen. The town of Bautzen stood on a plateau overlooking the river Spree, and at the top of this plateau was the Ortenburg Castle surrounded by the medieval city walls. Other places that would have their moment of fame during the fighting were Niesky, Kamenz, Königswartha, Bischofwerda and Hoyerswerda. Finally, let us remember that around the city of Bautzen there were several smaller towns that dotted the entire area and that today are mostly included within Bautzen as districts. We are referring to Stiebitz, Burk, Teichnitz, Oberkaina, Niederkaina, etc.

▲ The old city center of Bautzen in 1940, a city of 40,000 inhabitants, capital of Upper Lusatia, Saxony.

▲ Grenadiers of the 1st Armored Parachute Division "Hermann Göring" after a battle in a small village near Bautzen during the last days of April 1945. In the background is one of the Panzer IV tanks of the powerful Luftwaffe unit.

▼ Oberstleutnant Karl Rossman with his Iron Cross around his neck chats with the commander of the 2nd Company of his Battalion (Gerhard Tschierschwitz) and another officer with his Panther of the 1st Battalion of the Armored Regiment of the 1st Armored Parachute Division "Hermann Göring". On 19 April with the 17 tanks of his battalion he managed to deal a heavy blow to the Polish 1st Armored Corps, destroying at least 43 tanks and capturing another 12 intact.

THE PRECEDENTS OF THE BATTLE: THE BREAKING OF THE NEISSE DEFENSIVE LINE IN APRIL 1945

Although the Battle of Bautzen itself took place between 21 and 26 April 1945 and lasted until 30 April with some sporadic fighting both in the town itself and in the surrounding area, it is necessary to relate the preceding events that occurred as a result of the fighting on the southern flank of the Spremberg-Torgau Offensive (also known as Operation Lusatia) launched by the Red Army from the line of the Neisse River on 16 April 1945.

In the weeks leading up to the April 16 attack Bautzen, like the town of Weissenberg a little further east, had become a fortified location. When the enemy attack came, the two towns were to serve as breakwaters and bases from which to launch counterattacks, as had been decided in other places such as the famous Breslau. In Bautzen the commander of the garrison, Oberst Hoepke, had about 3,000 men. These troops were Volkssturm battalions, antiaircraft battalions, territorial units, a punishment company of the 4th Panzer Army, company remnants of the 1244th Grenadier Regiment, and about 200 men of the 10th SS Panzer Division "Frundsberg."

Soviet activity had increased along the front line in the days leading up to the attack of the Neisse defensive line; as early as the 14th, Soviet mortar and artillery fire had been directed toward the areas the Soviets had targeted along the Neisse. The situation clearly portended an imminent attack, as evidenced by the fact that Soviet reconnaissance forces also began building bridges to cross the river on the afternoon of 14 April along the Soviets' planned lines of advance. On April 15, several Luftwaffe air reconnaissance exercises revealed that the Soviets were gathering more and more troops and equipment in their deployment areas near the Neisse River. During these aerial reconnaissances, movement of artillery pieces positioned about 10 km from the front line was also noted. The Germans, for their part, in addition to the expected main Soviet attack, understood that several secondary attacks would most likely be carried out, but it was not known with certainty where the main attack would be carried out. The German High Command was trying to find out what the main Soviet line of advance would be, the doubt was whether they would attack along the Rothenburg-Bautzen axis, or whether the attack would take place along the Cottbus-Spremberg line. Finally, contrary to the expectations of the Germans, Koniev's main attack was launched between Cottbus and Spremberg and not between Rothenburg-Bautzen (on this axis, which was the one foreseen by the Germans as the main one, there was still a Soviet attack, although secondary). In spite of this, already on April 14 German troops had sufficient information to suspect with certainty that the main attack in this area of the Neisse River could have hit mainly the right flank of the "Brandenburg" division within a period of time not exceeding 24-36 hours.

DAY 16. SUNDAY

Faced with this situation of imminent danger in the area, the 1st Armored Parachute Division "Hermann Göring", was released from its reserve status and transferred by train to Görlitz where it was placed in the front line between the "Brandenburg" Division and the 72nd Infantry Division during the morning of 16 April. Recall that in the very early hours of dawn on April 16, 1945, Zhukov's forces (the 1st Belorussian Front) simultaneously with those located further south, corresponding to the seven armies of Marshal Koniev's 1st Ukrainian Front, began the offensive, which would finally target the city of Berlin. As we commented earlier, Zhukov's troops had been stopped on the heights of Seelow, while the southernmost flank of Koniev's men's advance would be involved in bloody fighting in the target area of Bautzen.

Koniev's main attack was directed at the front line between the 5th Army Corps and Panzer-Korps "Grossdeutschland." This area south of Forst and north of Muskau was very good terrain for the Soviet attack, and although it was flanked to the south by the Muskau Forest, there were a number of roads and highways laid out in the area that could easily connect Breslau or Dresden with Berlin. Thanks to the magnificent German road network, Koniev, once caught up with the Red Army, could, if necessary, move his troops north or south with some ease. Faced with the impressive power of the Soviet deployment, Hitler and his general staff realized that the highways could be too easy a line of advancement for the Soviets, so on April 15 they decided to order the destruction of the highways that maintained communication between Berlin and Forst, but kept intact the highways that ran from east to west; roads that would later play an important role in the events we are narrating. In the German zone, defending this area was the 342nd Infantry Division, a combat group (Kampfgruppe) of the 545th Volksgrenadier Division; while the 21st Panzer Division remained in the OKH reserve near the town of Spremberg. The remaining mobile divisions were in reserve further south of the 4th Panzer Army's right wing, where Schörner awaited the Soviet advance. The secondary Soviet attack in the direction of Rothenburg-Bautzen would place his forces in a position on the southern flank of the 4th Panzer Army, allowing them to surround most of the Central Army Group's mobile troops.

Koniev launched his attack on Neisse at exactly 6:10 a.m. (Moscow time) on April 16. Marshal Koniev tried to "split" the German defenses with his artillery, especially in the areas where he had planned his two attack directives. For his northern zone, with the intention of ending the siege on Berlin, he

▲ Oberstleutnant Karl Rossman's Panther of the 1st Parachute Armoured Division "Hermann Göring" lying in wait for its prey. This powerful tank model was responsible for most of the losses suffered by Polish and Soviet armored units during the Battle of Bautzen.

would march his main force consisting of the 3rd and 4th Armored Guard Armies, as well as the 13th, 3rd, and 5th Guard Corps. In its southern zone, with Dresden as its objective, the 52nd and 2nd Polish Armies would have marched. The Soviet attack devastated the two German divisions defending the main advance zone. The 545th Volksgrenadier Division was split into two groups, with most of its troops pushed south. The 342nd Infantry Division was virtually destroyed despite putting up fierce resistance. The survivors of the 342nd Infantry Division headed north in the direction of the Berlin-Breslau freeway, but they were subjected to continuous attack by Soviet vanguards, so that eventually the remnants of this German unit were reduced to a small fighting group. The superiority of the armored troops deployed by the Soviets allowed them to quickly overcome the German defensive lines, forcing them to retreat. In fact, in the first 24 hours of the operation, Koniev's troops managed to reach the Spree River.

The entire Soviet attack was also continuously supported by at least 1,500 Soviet Air Force aircraft departures. The direction of the secondary Soviet attack along the Rothenburg-Bautzen line began to be carried out a little farther south by the 7th Guard Mechanized Corps, the 2nd and 52nd Polish Armies. This combined force was ordered to advance westward to Dresden, although its main mission was to guard the southern flank of the main troops that would then head for Berlin.

The attack against the German defensive line was preceded by intense artillery fire for two hours against the German defenses. Of course, supporting the Soviet artillery were the Red Army's attack aircraft. This artillery preparation was followed by the massive Soviet attack, the main efforts of which involved Penzig and Rothenburg between Muskau and Forst. Initially, the Germans estimated that the attack consisted of four Soviet Groups and two armored armies.

The Polish 2nd Army, which would become one of the key players in our history, had been assigned under the operational command of the 1st Ukrainian Front and had the secondary task of advancing through Saxony and eliminating pockets of resistance with Soviet assistance. The purpose was to cover Koniev's main force in his attack on Berlin from the south of the capital; thus the aforementioned 2nd Polish Army was used as a spearhead for Saxon territory flanked on the right by the 5th Guard Army (Soviet) and on the left by the 7th Mechanized Corps (also Soviet).

In the first hours of the joint Soviet-Polish attack, the resistance of the German troops of the Central Army Group deployed on the banks of the Neisse, despite their combativeness, proved insufficient, causing their collapse after a short but fierce battle. The German troops, however, managed to retreat in an orderly fashion, always keeping an eye on the enemy's advance.

While the main force of the 1st Ukrainian Front broke through the German front near Forst and Bad Muskau and immediately headed for Berlin, the other Soviet spearhead headed for Dresden.

The "Brandenburg" Division was deployed in the advance zone of the Polish 2nd Army, as well as in that of part of the 52nd Army. The combined Soviet-Polish attack hit half of the "Brandenburg" Panzergrenadier Division, which at the time was still unaware that it was Polish troops attacking them. The first troops to cross the Neisse were the 254th Soviet Rifle Division and the 7th, 8th and 9th Polish Infantry Divisions, which quickly entered into combat against the "Brandenburgers" who defended themselves tenaciously. Many of the defenders were quickly "swallowed up" by the vanguard of the attackers, so after recovering from the first blow, many of these German soldiers began to move south, trying to re-establish a new line of defense. The attack of the Soviets was not a surprise for the soldiers of the Panzer Division "Brandenburg", because, as we said, it was clear that it would happen sooner or later. Moreover, they knew that the Neisse was not a real obstacle for the Soviets, since this river, in some areas, is only 15 m wide with a depth of no more than 1 m.

During the morning of the 16th the Soviets launched their main attack and hit the 2nd Hunter Reg-

▲ An Sd.Kfz 7 transport vehicle destroyed by a Soviet air raid in January 1945. This vehicle belonging to the 1st Armored Parachute Division "Hermann Göring" carries an 88 mm cannon in its trailer.

▼ The command Panther (Befehlspanther) numbered R01 of Oberstleutnant Karl Rossman advances through difficult terrain. When in the right hands, this tank was a tough match for any of the modern Soviet-made tanks such as the IS-2 or T-34/85.

iment of the Panzergrenadier Division "Brandenburg" in their positions in the forest southeast of Kahle Meile, near the railway line between Biehain and Zentendorf. The first battalion of this unit was hit hard by the Soviets. At about 5:00 a.m., the "Brandenburg" troops that had been attacked by the Soviets attempted to assemble and redraw a stable defensive line, but intense Soviet artillery fire that lasted until 7:45 a.m. prevented them from doing so. Thanks to their artillery, the Soviets managed to surround parts of the 1st Battalion of the 2nd Hunter Regiment of the "Brandenburg" (the units most affected by the Soviet attacks were the 1st Company and the 5th Heavy Company, which, having no possibility of escape, were finally captured). The situation was chaotic and in the afternoon of April 16 the remaining troops of the 2nd Hunter Regiment had to retreat back to the railway station of Kodersdorf where they formed a small defensive line that tried in vain to stop the attacking troops. Nevertheless, the German resistance pushed the 10th Polish Infantry Division to remain "stuck" in the attempt to advance westward.

Shortly after the beginning of the attack, and soon after, the participating divisions realized how difficult it would be to reach their objective, since the Russians had guarded their southern flank very well thinking of a possible attack by the German forces located in the area south of their line of advance. The German units found everywhere enemy tanks and anti-tank guns that prevented them from advancing. The German armored cars fought every kilometer to advance northward, but in the end they could not break through the Soviet lines to restore the German defense lines.

The advance of the 5th Guard Army westward toward Bautzen, with troops from the 2nd Polish Army and the 7th Guard Mechanized Corps escorting it, further aggravated the situation of the battered German units, as it would lead to a concentration of German troops where the Panzer-Korps Grossdeutschland, a Kampfgruppe (battle group) of the 545th Volksgrenadier Division, the 464th Division, the 615th z. b.V. and elements of the 1st "Brandenburg" Hunter Regiment. The situation in the afternoon of 16 to 17 was chaotic and the various units of the Panzer-Grenadier Division "Brandenburg" had been separated from each other and these in turn had been separated from the Panzer-Korps "Grossdeutschland" and the 4th Panzer Army.

Each battalion of the two fighter regiments (Jäger-Regiment) of the "Brandenburg" fought separately without contact with each other; the line of defense in the Neisse had been completely destroyed and the soldiers of the division were trying to survive against Soviet attacks. The 1st Battalion of the 2nd Hunter Regiment of the "Brandenburg" (Jäger-Reggiment 2) had been decimated and the survivors were trying to reach the German lines and rejoin them. The 2nd Battalion of the 1st "Brandenburg" Hunters Regiment (Jäger-Regiment 1) reached the forest east of Hähnichen in its retreat north, where it encountered elements of the 615th Z.b.V. Division that were retreating south (these troops along with the Panzer-Korps Grossdeutschland are the ones that would soon be pocketed by the rapid enemy advance). Meanwhile, on the right flank, the 1st Armored Parachute Division "Hermann Göring" was also being heavily hit by Soviet armored troops. Faced with this situation, the high command of the 4th Panzer Army had to reorganize immediately because most of its units had completely scattered.

By late afternoon, the advance of the attacking troops was about 8 kilometers long and 15 kilometers deep inside the German defensive lines. By the end of the day, the Soviets, thanks to other secondary attacks in the area, had hit the defensive front controlled by the Panzergrenadier Division "Brandenburg" very hard, the 545th Volksgrenadier Division was divided (as we said) and the Armored Parachute Division 1 "Hermann Göring" was already occupying its front line deployment area. In fact, for several hours, they had to face heavy fighting in the area of Zodel, just 8 km south of Görlitz, where they destroyed 31 Soviet tanks.

DAY 17. MONDAY.

After the first day of the advance, the Soviet-Polish troops succeeded in destroying the few defensive lines that the Germans had managed to establish north of the city of Görlitz. As on the previous day, the Soviet advance appeared unstoppable and the Germans had to retreat again towards the west, towards Dresden. But little by little the left flank of the Soviet-Polish advance was becoming more and more unguarded in enemy territory due to the desire to advance as fast as possible toward their objectives in Dresden and on the Elbe River.

The headquarters of Panzer-Korps "Grossdeutschland" had lost all communication with Panzer-Grenadier Division "Brandenburg". Soviet armored troops of the 7th Guard Mechanized Corps advanced with forces equivalent to a battalion through the gap created in the lines of the 1st Hunter Regiment "Brandenburg" and the 2nd Hunter Regiment "Brandenburg". At least 10 Soviet tanks reached the town of Spree, beyond the main line of the "Brandenburg".

Other elements of Soviet mechanized troops reached the left flank of the 2nd "Brandenburg" Hunter Regiment. The Polish 2nd Army quickly took advantage of the gap and crossed it by advancing westward along the wooded area between Reitschen and Niesky, where the Panzer-Korps "Grossdeutschland" was in danger of being encircled. The only divisions available to re-establish the defense of the right flank of the Panzer Korps "Grossdeutschland" were the 20th Panzer Division and the 1st Armored Parachute Division "Hermann Göring", stationed just south of Görlitz (they were joined by the Jagdpanzer-equipped Assault Artillery Brigade "Grossdeutschland", which went to Hähnichen to support the 1st Fighter Regiment of "Brandenburg"). Both divisions were already heading north to try to seal off the wide gap in the front. Further north on the left flank of Panzer-Korps "Grossdeutschland" was the 10th SS Panzer Division "Frundsberg," which was released from 4th Army reserve to counterattack the main advance line at Koniev, which threatened to break the 21st Panzer Division between Cottbus and Spremberg.

On April 17, Soviet forces of the 5th Army captured Weisswasser. The 1st Hunter Regiment of the "Brandenburg" retreated to Heidehauser, while the 615th Division z.b.V., the 2nd Battalion of the 1st Hunter Regiment of the "Brandenburg" and the 500th Engineer Battalion of the "Grossdeutschland" were separated from the rest of the "Brandenburg". The 2nd Battalion of the 2nd Regiment of Hunters of the "Brandenburg" was hit by Soviet troops, to which it put up a weak defense in the railway station of Kodersdorf and subsequently withdrew.

In the sector of the 1st Hunter Regiment of the "Brandenburg" the Soviet attack persisted and the German soldiers defended themselves with their panzerfaust in the nearby fighting, stationed among the ruins of the burning buildings. At noon the "Brandenburg" Armored Assault Engineer Battalion (specifically two of its Companies) withdrew toward Niesky and took up defensive positions in the area of the train station.

At about 15.00, the assault troops attacked the castle of Wehrkirch (only 5 kilometers from Niesky) with a formation of about 100 armored vehicles, their vanguard was formed by the powerful T-34, while the troops of the "Brandenburg" Armored Assault Engineer Battalion were stationed with 88 mm pieces and panzerfaust. After a bloody fight, the remains of at least 40 armored vehicles destroyed by the Germans could be seen. But this small victory did not stop the Soviets, who only a few hours later (around 9 p.m.), launched a rain of artillery shells that completely destroyed the castle and most of its defenders. After fighting all day in that area, the survivors tried to retreat to their own defensive lines established in the Muskauer forest, located near the castle between the towns of Niesky and Neuhoff.

On the nights of April 16-17 and 17-18, the German armored vanguard of the 1st Parachute Division "Hermann Göring," the 20th Panzer Division, the Panzergrenadier Division "Brandenburg" (which was still trying to regroup its troops after the previous day's withdrawal) and the 17th Infantry Division tried to continue their advance from the south to try to "close" the huge corridor the attackers had created, but were eventually stopped, not before destroying dozens of Russian tanks. The Soviets renewed their attack along the left flank of the 2nd Fighter Regiment "Brandenburg" of the 7th Guard Mechanized Corps. The entire 2nd Grenadier Regiment of the "Brandenburg" was about to be surrounded by the Soviet armored maneuver, but the situation was stabilized by an attack of the armored elements of the 1st Armored Parachute Division "Hermann Göring", which had launched a counterattack.

In order to allow Koniev to advance without risks in the rear of the attacks of the German troops, the Second Polish Army of General Świerczewski began the "cleaning" of the whole area near the Niesse to avoid the formation of heaps of German troops and led his men to the town of Niesky, which was captured and subjected to acts of pillage by the Red Army troops. Some of the German troops that had been driven out of their defensive positions retreated in the direction of Dresden (the capital of Saxony). It was clear that the mission designated by Marshal Koniev for the Polish unit was to protect the southern flank of the main advance of the 1st Ukrainian Front, which corresponded to the Dresden-Bautzen-Niesky line.

The situation was very favorable to the Russians according to General Świerczewski, so he did not hesitate to extend his lines to move even faster on Dresden, the final objective, and with the city of Bautzen in the center. But the Polish general's inadequate assessment of the overall situation, as well as his underestimation of the German troops still in the area, would soon turn against him and his Second Polish Army. Nor can we forget that the aggressive character of the Polish leader did not help his subordinates to dare in any case to contradict their superior or to make any decision independently.

On the German side, all that remained was to reorganize and re-establish a new line of defense that would stop the aggressors and later, if possible, attack them and force them to retreat. Multiple scenes of panic, courage, desperation, and daring occurred among the German units. Probably the Panzergrenadier Division "Brandenburg" was one of those that did the most in the joint Soviet-Polish effort. During the fighting until the 17th, the men of the "Brandenburg" showed great resistance after two days of total enemy superiority and confusion, as communications between the various units were inadequate due to the massive disruption between the German lines of the Poles and Soviets. The rapid march of the Poles and Soviets westward meant that on numerous occasions they were trapped behind their own lines where German troops held out.

DAY 18. TUESDAY

The situation was becoming more complicated in the southern area of the Soviet advance line and the various German units, the 1st Parachute Armored Division "Hermann Göring", the 20th Panzer Division, the Panzer Grenade Division "Brandenburg" and the 17th Infantry Division faced not only containment forces but also numerous counterattacks supported by armored vehicles. These southward attacks by Red Army troops forced the German units to retreat from the attack into defensive positions. The "Brandenburg" armored units deployed between Spreefurt and Kodesdorf fought bravely against the

▲ The wreckage after the battle near Bautzen. In the foreground there is a dead German soldier, possibly after being hit by the Kubelwagen he was traveling on (bottom of image) and attempting to escape on foot. From waralbum.ru

▼ A Panther Ausf G. tank of the "Frundsberg" Division destroyed by Soviet fire near Cottbus in April 1945. Only 200 men without tanks from this unit, who had been left behind after the unit's march north, took part in the fighting for Bautzen. This was the only contribution of an SS division in that battle; the bulk of the fighting was carried by army and Luftwaffe units.

▲ Troops of the Polish 21st Army march merrily and carefree through the Saxon landscape toward Dresden. They would soon realize that the war was far from over.

▼ An IS-2 of the Polish 4th Armored Regiment crosses a log bridge in April 1945. The Soviets supplied the Polish (pro-Soviet) Army with important armored vehicles including these modern heavy tanks. Unknown origin.

▲ A Jagdpanzer IV used by the "Grossdeutschland" assault artillery brigade. Together with Panther tanks, they were the most numerous armored vehicles in the German arsenal during the battle for Bautzen.

attacks of the troops supported by a large number of T-34/85 and IS-2. The German artillery itself had to fire on a strip of land where the attackers were confused with the defenders. The attempt to seal off the Russian attack had definitely failed.

At Spreeberg Castle, where the headquarters of the Army Corps was located, the German troops led by Major Theodor Bethke (the staff officer in charge) carried out an attack against the enemy formations advancing in their area. As many men as possible were needed to try to stem the flooding of the "red tide" in eastern Saxony.

It was between Görlitz and Niesky that the Soviet-Polish troops made their main effort to advance towards Dresden. In their advance towards the Saxon capital, General Karol Świerczewski ordered the 8th Infantry Division and the 1st Armored Corps (belonging to the 2nd Polish Army) to engage the remaining German formations deployed to the south to force them to withdraw from the area of operations. In the meantime, the 5th, 7th, 9th and 10th Infantry Divisions (the remaining units of the Polish 2nd Army) would take up position north of the town of Bautzen after crossing Weissenberg, surrounding some German formations that remained behind the Soviet lines, such as in the area near the town of Muskauer. Weissenberg was captured by the Soviet 7th Mechanized Guard Corps on April 18. The 294th Rifle Division was left at Weissenberg as a garrison of the town to keep the troop crossing open in an east-west direction allowing the rest of the Mechanized Corps to advance toward Bautzen.

At 9:00 a.m., the 26th Mechanized Brigade advanced at full speed and took Buchholz, from where its armorers then attacked the village of Wasserkretzscham, just a couple of kilometers from Weissenberg. The defenders of the village, the Volkssturm troops, managed to destroy some T-34/85s with their panzerfausts, but they could not cope with the enormous power of the attackers.

It was necessary to increase the pressure on the Germans, so Marshal Koniev ordered the Polish 2nd Army to "open" its ranks to allow the 7th Mechanized Guard Corps in the Jänkendorf area to join the vanguard of attack. Therefore, this same April 18, earlier than expected, the garrison troops deployed at Weissenberg suddenly found themselves with the Russian vanguard in front. After breaking through

▲ Between April 17 and 18, 1945 a bloody battle was fought over the town of Niesky involving Polish troops of the 2nd Army (referred to in this photograph). The photo shows a pair of Polish soldiers firing a Soviet-made Maxim machine gun behind a destroyed 75mm German Pak 40 cannon.

▲ Sanitary half-track Sd.Kfz. 251/8 sanitary half-track belonging to the 1st Armored Parachute Division "Hermann Göring" during the fighting on the Eastern Front in defense of East Prussia.

▼ A pair of ISU -122 heavy self-propelled guns belonging to the 1st Ukrainian Front moving along the front line in 1945. These armored vehicles were very dangerous due to the large caliber of their main gun. From waralbum.ru

▲ Soldiers belonging to the 7th Infantry Division of the Polish 2nd Army in early April 1945, prior to the attack on the Neisse Line.

the German front at Rothenburg, the 7th Mechanized Guard Corps in the southern wing of the Russian forces headed for Dresden and immediately sent forces toward Weissenberg. On the very morning of April 18, after attacking Weissenberg from all sides simultaneously, they occupied the town at about 9:30 a.m. Resistance in this town, as the German high command had anticipated, was not very intense. The surviving troops that had defended the city, supported by an 88 mm cannon, tried to escape from the city through the Soviet lines. Once the enclave was captured, the victorious Red Army men continued their advance along the Reich Highway towards Bautzen.

Faced with advancing enemy troops, the Germans decided to blow up the bridge over the Löbauer River in an attempt to slow down the advancing Soviets in some way. At that critical moment, Ju 87 G-2 tank destroyers armed with two 37mm cannons made their appearance. These old, but still dangerous aircraft were commanded by Obstlt. Hans Ulrich Rudel (the most decorated German military officer during the entire war). The planes were equipped with two 37 mm cannons firing tungsten-tipped projectiles, which were lethal against tanks that were less armored on top (37 mm projectiles were capable of piercing 95 mm of armor at 600 meters and up to 140 mm at 100 meters). The aircraft belonged to the III./SG 2 "Immelmann" (specifically 10.(Pz)/SG 2), which was at the time the only unit in the entire Luftwaffe that still flew the Ju 87 "Stuka". The Ju 87 "tank hunters" took a heavy toll on the Soviets, as they managed to destroy 6 enemy tanks and immobilize at least 3 more (in total the III./SG 2 managed to destroy 26 enemy tanks during the battles for Bautzen, of which its commander-in-chief, Rudel, added 3 more to his victories); however, due to the large amount of material assets and the Soviets' sky command, they were unable to stop such an offensive. The successes in the Stukas' attacks were also aided by the fact that the areas through which the Polish-Soviets advanced in the Bautzen area abounded with open and clear areas that allowed their veteran pilots to hone their aim even better.

The advance of the 7th Guards Mechanized Corps was very fast. In fact, the 26th Mechanized Guard Brigade was using the highway to approach Bautzen, while the 24th Mechanized Guard Brigade was approaching the city from positions a little south of the highway.

At Gröditz, around noon, Soviet tanks accompanied by 5 infantry trucks began to arrive. The situation

▲ A soldier reloads one of the 37mm cannons with which ace Heinz Ulrich Rudel's Stukas were armed in SG 2. These tungsten-tipped projectiles were lethal against the tanks.

▼ Uno degli Stukas obsoleti ma ancora pericolosi rivali grazie ai suoi cannoni da 37 mm, appartenente al III./SG 2 "Immelmann" (nello specifico 10.(Pz)/SG 2); l'unica unità di tutta la Luftwaffe che ancora volava con lo Ju 87 "Stuka". Bundesarchiv

was becoming critical for the troops in Bautzen, so Oberst Dietrich Hoepke gave the order to blow up the freeway bridge over the Oehna and to move his staff to the imposing Ortenburg castle, which from its height dominated the town and its surroundings.

At dusk on April 18, the first elements of the 24th and 26th Mechanized Brigades reached the eastern outskirts of Bautzen near the airport. The city was already within sight of the Red Army troops, and it did not take long for the first fighting, which occurred to the east of the city as the 24th Guards Mechanized Brigade approached the Bautzen-Litten airfield.

The fierce defense of the airfield was led by Major Schule (who had received explicit orders to this effect from Oberst Dietrich Hoepke, in order to gain time to correctly position the artillery pieces in support of Flak-Abteilung 383, positioned at Schafberg). The defense raised by the anti-tank unit of Volkssturm-Bataillone 27/33 under the command of Kompagnieführer Hans Zeller, succeeded in hitting the first enemy troops that arrived in Bautzen (belonging to the 24th Guards Mechanized Brigade) thanks to small anti-tank commandos, even if immediately afterwards the Soviet attacks to take the airport began. After that, and seeing that the defense of the airport was impossible to maintain, they proceeded to blow up the local ammunition depot, as well as the main hangar, and quickly the Volkssturm retreated to Neupurschwitz. But when the unsuspecting Soviets penetrated the airfield they destroyed at least three anti-aircraft guns and about 20 aircraft of different types that still remained on the airfield (most likely the Stuka planes of SG 2 took off from its runways to carry out selective attacks against the attacking armored vehicles while it was still in German hands), but they still received fire from the 88 mm guns belonging to the heavy battery; at least 3 Russian trucks were destroyed.

In the city Hoepke ordered the immediate evacuation of civilians, but this was not completed definitively, as we shall see. Shortly after the fall of the airfield, 2 T-34/85 of the 13th Armored Regiment of the Guard advanced accompanied by mounted troops of the 24th Mechanized Brigade of the Guard and attempted to reach Schafberg just outside the town at nightfall. At about 10 p.m., the 13th Armored Regiment of the 24th Guards Mechanized Brigade made contact with the Bautzen defensive network, which they fired on in the dark of night with their tanks.

Later in the night, a fierce fight for Schafberg took place involving the men of the German Punitive Company of the 4th Panzer Army (who had just taken their defensive positions just an hour before the Soviet attack) in which the defenders refused to flee and resisted to the last. The hill they were defending fell to the Russians at about 11:00 pm. During these offensive movements, the Soviets also captured the Carolagarten and Nadelwitz crossroads. Between 2:00 a.m. and 3:00 a.m. on the morning of April 19, elements of the 24th Guards Mechanized Brigade moved south and began to reach the town near the König Albert military training base where Hitler Youth boys, armed with two or three panzerfausts each and supported by two 88mm guns, temporarily held the Soviets at bay.

By the end of the 18th, the units of the Polish 2nd Army and 52nd Army were positioned as follows:

The Polish 2nd Army, having broken through the first and second German defensive lines, was fighting along the Senitz- Spreutz- Diehsa line, having penetrated about 20 km into enemy territory.

The 1st Armored Corps, which had fought on April 18 in the Spreutz sector, had left its infantry about 6 km behind. By the end of the day, fighting was taking place in the Forstgen area.

The 1st Guards Cavalry Corps, which had fought south of Spreutz, had also been separated from its infantry by 6 km and was fighting in the Ober Prauske area and in the woods north of Ober Prauske.

▲ Left emblem used by the 20th Panzer Division between 1943 and 1945. The armored vehicles of this division played an important role during the various battles in Eastern Saxony. Right emblem of the swooping eagle of the 1st Armored Parachute Division "Hermann Göring". Together with the "Brandenburg", they were the two German divisions on which the German victory at the Battle of Bautzen was built. Public Domain.

▼ Emblem of the Panzer-Grenadier Division "Brandenburg". As you can see it is based on the emblem of its parent unit, the "Grossdeutschland" Division. Public Domain.

The spearhead of the 52nd Army was entering along the Zerichen-Kodersdorf-Zodel-Penzig line, having penetrated 12 km deep into the German defense.

The 7th Guards Mechanized Corps, which had been fighting in the Diehsa area along with the 254th Rifle Division, had separated from its infantry by about 22 km and managed to reach the third German defensive line. By the end of the day, fighting was taking place on the Rakel-Kotitz-Weissenberg line. Together, the attack group of the Polish 2nd Army and the 52nd Army had managed, after breaking through the Neisse defensive line, to lead its troops in the direction of Bautzen-Dresden.

Against these two Soviet-Polish attacking forces, the following German forces were activated: the Brandenburg Panzer-Grenadier Division, the 615th z.b.V. Division and about 10 independent battalions. Immediately, the 20th Panzer Division and the 1st Parachute Armored Division "Hermann Göring" were released from the reserve of Army Group Center. These two units appeared at the end of the 18th in the area north of Görlitz, receiving orders to move north and be transferred to the right flank of the German 17th Army. The 464th German Infantry Division had been moved from the Dresden area to the Richen area to engage the forces of the Polish 2nd Army. The 404th and 193rd Infantry Divisions, in turn, were transferred from the Dresden area to augment the defensive line along the line between Görlitz and Lauban, about 22 kilometers southeast of Görlitz.

The German high command of the 4th Army considered that the most important option would be to attack the southern flank of the 52nd Army on the Spremberg-Weisswasser axis with the powerful armored forces they had managed to mass in the Görlitz area. If everything had gone according to the best predictions, they would have created a major crisis in the advance of the 1st Ukrainian Front against South Berlin. In the end it was decided that April 19 would be the date for the beginning of the German counterattack.

DAY 19. WEDNESDAY.

Korchagine was aware of the German defensive positions, so they began to attack Bautzen on April 19 and while the 24th Guards Mechanized Brigade headed directly toward the city from the east (following the road from Weissenberg), the city was surrounded from the north by the 26th Guards Mechanized Brigade (from its positions on the road at Burk level it was ordered to attack along the highway and then head south) and from the south by the 25th Guards Mechanized Brigade and the 57th Armored Brigade. In addition, the presence of the 254th Rifle Division with its three regiments (929th 933rd and 936th) was requested to support the final blow against the population. Korchagine thought that by attacking Bautzen from three different points, the German resistance would be forced to surrender. In addition, the attacking forces were able to establish a bridgehead across the Spree River to block any possibility of German reinforcements arriving. It was clearly an unequal fight, as the defenders had no chance against such a large number of opponents. The administrative personnel stationed in Bautzen, as well as the boys of the Hitler Youth, had to take up arms and join their comrades in the defense.

The main assault on the town was carried out by the 24th Brigade of the Mechanized Guard, which was ordered to attack towards the Löbauer Street and continue in the direction of the castle (this unit was supported by troops from the 254th Rifle Division). At 04:00 on 19 April, the Soviets attempted to break the resistance of the defenders with a 15-minute artillery bombardment of the eastern part

▲ Image of the Altstadt bridge in the city of Görlitz in 1907. The 4th Armored Army was deployed between Görlitz and Cottbus to defend the Neisse line against the Red Army. Public Domain

of the town. Immediately thereafter, 10 T-34/85s of the 13th Guards Armored Regiment were launched against the German defenses at Nadelwitz, in that case supported by the men of the 3rd Company of Volkssturm-Bataillone 27/32. The tanks, supported by infantry, overwhelmed that defensive line and about 30 Volkssturm were captured, while a handful of them managed to escape to friendly positions in the Kant barracks. There they joined their defenders, which consisted of a company from the 1459th Fortress Infantry Battalion and the personnel of a Flak battalion (Flak-Abteilung). The total number of men, counting the survivors of the newly arrived 3rd Company of Volkssturm-Bataillone 27/32nd, amounted to only 105 men and completely devoid of heavy weapons. Again the Soviets showed their strength and subjected the barracks to heavy artillery, tank and mortar fire, after which the Soviet infantrymen charged at 10:15. The fighting was brutal and in a short time more than half of the defenders were put out of action. In fact, the survivors of the Company of the 1459th Fortress Infantry Battalion fled, leaving behind the men of the Flak and some Volkssturm who in the meantime had to keep the attackers "at bay". Completely besieged, the men who were still able to escape from the barracks, after a couple of hours tried to make a sortie. The result was that only 5 officers and 20 soldiers belonging to the staff of the Flak battalion managed to escape from there, as the Soviets and especially their snipers riddled them with all kinds of weapons from their hidden positions. These 25 survivors in their escape managed to reach the positions of a Company of the 1461st Fortress Infantry Battalion positioned nearby. Shortly afterwards, this company, reinforced by the 25 men, launched a small counter-attack on Löbauer Street which was completely suppressed by Soviet artillery pieces (the leader of the unit, Major Schober, was killed when a panzerfaust fired at a T-34/85 bounced off a fence and exploded next to him).

At the same time, for its part, the 215th Armored Regiment of the 26th Guards Mechanized Brigade (the vanguard of the 26th Guards Mechanized Brigade) captured Niederkain and moved northwest to reach Burk by mid-morning, where it was met by defenders with 37mm fire. But the significant imbalance between attackers and defenders allowed the German artillery to be quickly silenced with the support of the 215th Armored Regiment. After that, the Soviets advanced to take the heights of Berk, where they captured two artillery pieces, and from where they controlled the banks of the Spree.

At the same time, around 9:00 a.m., the 24th Mechanized Brigade captured the supply depots located on Löbauer Street, but always facing increasingly fierce resistance.

To the south, the 25th Guards Mechanized Brigade and the 57th Guards Armored Brigade advanced at high speed toward the "Husar" military training base and reached the highway at Neusalzaer Street. The Soviet attack from the south was rapid and unexpected by German troops, so that soon there were small gaps in the defensive line and some German troops were isolated and swallowed up by the Soviet advance. The progress of the 25th Guards Mechanized Brigade and the 57th Armored Brigade southward was easier because of their tanks. Thanks to their T-34/85 they took the station and penetrated as far as Neusalzaer Street. The German resistance was total, even the small counterattacks, such as the one that, against the Soviet troops of these two units, was carried out by the troops of the 54th Anti-Aircraft Regiment (FlaK) under the command of Oberstleutnant Tödt. The result was disastrous for the Germans who found themselves facing the enormous Soviet armored power.

The advance of the Soviets was similar to a steamroller that climbed little by little towards the high center of the city, breaking one by one the German defensive positions that they found. The defenders tried at the cost of their lives to stop the enemy armored advance; in these actions some of the Hitler Youth boys had the opportunity to fire their panzerfausts. As the day progressed, the Russians entered

▲ Soviet soldiers are busy loading a battery of Soviet Katiushka missiles. Another similar vehicle can be seen in the background. The firepower of these vehicles was responsible, along with conventional artillery, for the virtual destruction of German defenses on the Neisse on April 16, 1945. Public Domain

▼ Group of motorcyclists belonging to the Polish 2nd Army during its intervention in Eastern Saxony in April 1945, recognizable by their distinctive cap called a czapka. The unit is equipped with American Harley-Davidson motorcycles, delivered to the Soviet Union as part of a loan treaty. Public Domain

▲ Polish 2nd Army artillery units cross a pontoon bridge over the Neisse between April 16 or 17, 1945. An M-30 122 mm howitzer is seen being towed by an American-made Studebaker US-6 truck. Yet another sign of the large amount of British or American equipment that served in the ranks of the Red Army thanks to the Lend-Lease treaty. Public Domain

▼ Several Panther tanks belonging to the 20th Panzer Division in the fall of 1944 while deployed in Romania. A few months later, after being adequately reinforced, the panzer division participated in the fighting for Bautzen with great success. Public Domain

the city and gradually forced the defenders to retreat, who fought relentlessly for every meter of Bautzen. At about 9 p.m., in the confusion of the fighting, the men of Volkssturm-Bataillone 27/32 who were still standing retreated to the station, unaware that it had been in enemy hands for several hours. In total, it is estimated that 120 men were captured by the Russians and subsequently evacuated to the rear (to Weigersdorf), being left in command of a Polish unit. These men, two days later, were all executed by the Poles on a farm in Niederkaina, coinciding with the German advance from the south on Bautzen.

The ring around the town was tightening by the hour, but the Russian pincer was not yet completely closed on the Saxon town. The situation changed when the Polish 3rd Armored Brigade, which was advancing north of Bautzen behind units of the Soviet 7th Mechanized Guard Corps, turned south to attack and cut the highway to Dresden in the vicinity of Döbschke in order to hit Bautzen from the north and thus complete the encirclement.

While the fighting in the streets of Bautzen steadily increased the number of casualties on both sides, on the outskirts of the city the situation was changing dramatically. The Soviet advance had been so rapid that Korchagine had neglected his rear, now covered by the men of the Polish 2nd Army. For General Georg Jauer, head of Panzer-Korps "Grossdeutschland", this situation had not gone unnoticed, so it was immediately decided that this was the perfect time to strike at the rear of the 7th Guards Mechanized Corps. For this, the chosen troops were the 20th Panzer Division and the Armored Regiment of the 1st Armored Parachute Division "Hermann Göring". The objective was to reach the highway between Bautzen and Görlitz, which was not adequately covered by Polish troops, and to establish again a continuous front line in front of the enemy. With this attack from the south, the 7th Mechanized Guard Corps would have isolated itself from its comrades and would have been an easier enemy to hit. Jauer also felt it was appropriate to attack in a southerly direction with the 615th Z.b.V Division accompanied by the "Brandenburg" unit temporarily attached to it, with the intention of re-establishing a new front line between Panzer-Korps Grossdeutschland and LVII Panzer-Korps further south. The German pincer maneuver was beginning to affect Soviet and Polish units in that area.

At the same time, much of the southern flank of the Soviet-Polish troops in their advance through the Bautzen-Weissenberg area began to be hit with unusual force. Thus, 2 km east of Kodersdorf a bloody battle took place between the 1st Battalion of the Armoured Regiment of the 1st Parachute Armoured Division "Hermann Göring" (commanded by Oberstleutnant Rossmann) and the Polish 1st Armoured Corps (which had just been moved to the southern part of the Polish advance precisely to meet the German forces attacking them from that direction). The crews of the 17 Panther tanks of the parachute unit waiting for one of the Polish counterattacks (although at first the Germans thought it was a Soviet and not a Polish armored unit), waited for the enemy tanks up to 50 meters before receiving the order from Rossmann to open fire. The Poles followed the banks of the Schwarzer Schöps River without any kind of vigilance or proper tactical discipline, as if they were not in the middle of a war. During the 20 minutes of fighting that followed, at least 43 Polish tanks were destroyed and the rest of the Polish unit surrendered to the Germans. After the surrender, the men of the "Hermann Göring" captured 12 enemy tanks, including three or four vehicles of the mighty Josef Stalin 2 (perhaps 4), which would later be reused by the Germans after conveniently applying large German crosses to replace the insignia of the defeated. As we have been able to appreciate, even at this point in the war with almost everything already lost, the German armored forces still had the capability, proper tactical deployment and discipline to cause much damage to any enemy armored unit even in obvious numerical inferiority.

As a final result of stubborn German resistance, the Soviet attack in the southern direction had to be stopped, although Soviet forces were left in the area with the intention of "fixing" German units on the ground. But Schörner did not intend to sit still, so the 1st Parachute Armored Division "Hermann

▲ Polish troops of the 2nd Army on the march during fighting with the Germans in the second half of April 1945. Public Domain
▼ Soldiers of the 28th Infantry Regiment pose for the photographer in the town of Niesky on April 20, 1945. Public Domain

▲ Parade of the "triumphant" troops of the Polish 2nd Army in Melnik, Czech Republic, in May 1945. The performance of the Polish 2nd Army during the period from April 16 to the end of the war in Europe can be considered catastrophic despite being on the side of the victors. Public Domain

Göring" was withdrawn from the front and assigned to the Parachute Panzer-Korps located in the Bautzen area. Like the parachute unit, the 17th and 72nd Infantry Divisions were also withdrawn from the front and deployed further east, resting for the fighting to come. There would be no real rest for the 1st Armored Parachute Division "Hermann Göring", because in only 3 days (April 22) it would take part in the counterattack to liberate Bautzen, surrounded by the Soviets.

In addition to the Panther action of the "Hermann Göring", the 20th Panzer Division also launched a powerful attack from the Diehsa area that hit the southern flank of the enemy advance.

By the end of April 19, the troops of the 2nd Polish Army had advanced between 4 and 15 kilometers and had reached the Birckfere-Pribus-Zenitz-Daubitz-Kreba-Spreutz-Diehsa-Edernitz line. The 7th Guard Mechanized Corps together with the 254th Rifle Division, as mentioned above, had also reached the eastern hills of Bautzen and were causing great havoc among the defenders. In addition, the 10th SS Panzer Division "Frundsberg," the Führer-Begleit-Division, and the 344th Infantry Division had become trapped in a pocket at Spremberg (these troops were then subjected to continuous enemy attacks, only the Führer-Begleit-Division and the 344th Infantry Division managed to break the pocket of German troops in small groups by April 22); for its part, the 10th SS Panzer Division "Frundsberg" managed to escape with heavy losses but maintained its cohesion to finally reunite with friendly troops on April 26 northwest of Dresden.

DAY 20. THURSDAY

As we have already mentioned, the Soviet-Polish advance had been virtually unstoppable, which allowed the Red Army outposts to reach the outskirts of Bautzen on April 19 and begin to overwhelm its defenders from various points. After the capture of Niesky, the Poles had advanced victoriously

▲ A massive ISU-152 approaches the front. The Polish 2nd Army had more than 100 self-propelled tank destroyers, mainly SU-85s and ISU-152s. Public Domain

toward the Bautzen area, capturing the town of Weissenberg, and the Soviet advance led by the 7th Mechanized Corps entered the town on April 20. This move was aimed at completely securing the line south of Niesky.

In the course of the day the German positions diminished by the hour, but the city of Bautzen was fought to the death. The commander in chief of the "Festung" of Bautzen, Oberst Dietrich Hoepke, understood the futility of launching those small counterattacks against the Soviets as in the previous day, as they would have been fatal for most of the German troops involved. Therefore, he gave the order to withdraw the troops defending the outer perimeter of the city to retreat in an orderly fashion to the defensive belt located inside Bautzen.

The 26th mechanized brigade of the Guards advancing from Burk, at 4: 00 a.m. crossed the Spree and under heavy supporting fire from their artillery batteries and mortar fire, succeeded in capturing Teichnitz, which was defended by men belonging to Volkssturm-Bataillone 27/33 housed in the kindergarten near the base of the Ortenburg Castle plateau (well supplied with Italian-made panzerfausts and hand grenades but with a few shabby old French rifles and only 5 rounds per man).

Once the tanks managed to cross the Spree, they quickly halted their advance and the Soviets began to establish their small bridgehead by continuing to harass with sniper fire the Volksturm who were holding out at the aforementioned kindergarten. After the Soviets were reinforced by the 26th Polish Infantry Regiment, the men of the 3rd Company of the Volkssturm Battalion (Volkssturm-Bataillone 27/33) finally had to retreat in the direction of the castle.

For its part, the Soviet 24th Mechanized Brigade began to eliminate all enemies in its advance zone. The sawmill and the post office, among other buildings, were two of the targets of the Soviet armored vehicles, which were used as battering rams against the barricades and against the walls of the houses.

The Germans fought taking advantage of the destruction of the city and hid in the rubble, in the remains of the walls, in the basements, to attack the Soviet steel giants with their panzerfausts and the enemy infantry with their rifles, although the feat immediately appeared almost impossible. Thanks to 122mm rounds from the IS-2s, the Soviets were able to bring down a wall of the post office, through which the infantry entered and ended all German resistance. At that moment, the only resistance offered to the armored vehicles of the Soviet 24th Mechanized Brigade was the German troops repaired in the elementary school building.

▲ Along with the increasingly depleted armored units, the panzerfaust and panzerschreck (like the one carried by the infantryman in the photo) were the other main weapons in the fight against the countless tanks and self-propelled guns of the Soviets and Poles. Bundesarchiv_Bild_146-1985-092-29

Elsewhere in the city, as on the previous day, the fighting continued house by house, room by room, cellar by cellar; the fighting was fierce. Meanwhile, artillery fire had begun throughout the city and Russian snipers caused many casualties. South of Bautzen, the 57th Armored Brigade of the Guards had orders to secure the railway line and the national road (highway) No. 6. Around noon, the vanguard of this unit managed to enter the outskirts of Stiebitz (which would be taken at sunset), where to the southeast at least one T-34/85 managed to reach the railroad, cutting it off for good. The Soviets were in a hurry to close the encirclement of the city and that there was no possibility of escape of the German troops. Even at that time only 3.5 kilometers separated the formations of the 57th Guards Armored Brigade and the 26th Guards Mechanized Brigade in Teichnitz.

The situation inside Bautzen was critical for the defenders, but they still held their positions in the brewery, the high school building, and a few other locations. Already defending the inner ring, the German troops took advantage of the old medieval fortifications against the attackers' fire. In addition, the streets were filled with barricades and small fortifications trying to prevent the enemy armored advance. To add to the chaos, the hospital where at least 400 seriously wounded Germans were located was captured by the Soviets at dusk. Thanks to this Soviet attack, the state prison building (which was still in German hands) was completely cut off from its compatriots and surrounded by enemy troops, despite Hoepke's attempts to recapture them. The Volkssturm, the Hitler Youth and the 2nd level troops defending Bautzen, continued to do so even after hours of massive Soviet attack. The order was to hold out until the end, and so they were doing. At the gates of Ortenburg Castle there was a continuous movement of attacking troops supported by their armor and heavy mortar fire; the situation was becoming very difficult for the exhausted defenders of Bautzen.

Soviet attacks trying to break through the positions of the castle and the Schützenplatz were followed by small German counterattacks that managed to stop them momentarily. The losses sustained by the front-line men were replaced by the Hitler Youth (of the castle) and the men of Landesschützen Bataillone 992 (defending the eastern bank of the Spree River at the very base of the promontory where the castle was located). In fact, at 19:15, Oberst Hoepke gave the order to blow up the Kronprinz bridge, which would have completely cut off the survivors of the garrison from outside the city (and thus also the many civilians who had failed to evacuate the city, still estimated at about 5,000 despite the evacuation order). But before doing so, he allowed the removal of the men of the "Frundsberg" who were still in Bautzen (leaving their vehicles without fuel), as well as a number of Volkssturm elders (about two-thirds of the total Volkssturm men) who could no longer contribute to the defense.

Kolchagin did not want to waste any more time in capturing Bautzen, so he ordered a reinforced battalion to occupy Bischofswerda and Nierderputzkau, both southwest of Bautzen. At the same time, to the west of the town the 26th Polish Regiment of the 9th Infantry Division reached National Road 6 near Göda cutting its connection with Bautzen.

There was still a small pocket (the last) of resistance on the west bank of the town and it was occupied by the men of the 3rd Company of Volkssturm-Bataillone 27/33, but the Polish troops, with great aggression, forced them to retreat across the Seidauer Street Bridge.

After the almost complete capture of Bautzen (which was not completed because of two small pockets of German troops in the city that continued to resist the attackers) the desire of General Świerczewski was to continue the advance towards Dresden. We must remember that the main objective of the Polish unit was to prevent the German troops still remaining in the area south of Görlitz from attacking the southern flank of the advance of the 1st Ukrainian Front towards Berlin. If the Polish unit had remained in the area of Bautzen, perhaps now we would not be talking about the last German victory in the Second World War, but General Świerczewski decided to continue towards the Saxon capital, perhaps out of an eagerness to take, with the Polish troops, a large German capital (even if after the bombing suffered Dresden was now reduced to rubble in its almost entirety), separating himself from the initial plan of attack that had been established by Marshal Koniev.

Although the southern flank of the Polish advance was meeting serious resistance (they had reached the Baruth-Forstgen-Spreutz line), their flanks, central and northern, continued their advance of about 12-16 kilometers into German territory, reaching the Kuppatz-Heide-Milkel-Malkwitz line at the end of the day. For its part, the 52nd Army was in continuous contact along its entire front with the attacking units of the Görlitz Group of Forces.

Meanwhile, on the German side, Schörner wasted no time in building up his troops in the area near the city of Görlitz and in the Rheinbach region (he also added a new unit, the 72nd Infantry Division, which had withdrawn from the defensive line between Lauban and Penzig to join the Görlitz Group of Forces). From there, he planned to counterattack against the southern flank of the Polish unit, allowing him to somehow disrupt the southern front of the Soviet attack on the city of Berlin. Schörner's dif-ficult and theoretical objective, as we have already mentioned, was to break the encirclement of Wilhelm Busch's German 9th Army south of the Reich capital and subsequently to send his operational force against the encirclement of Berlin itself. Schörner's practical objective was simpler, as it was to gain time to allow the withdrawal of the maximum number of German units and civilians to the west.

Thus, General Fritz-Hübert Gräser launched his troops from south of Görlitz and into the Löbau region against the southern flank of the Polish 2nd Army, which was caught completely unprepared and with its lines stretched very thin as it made its way towards Dresden. Incomprehensibly, General Świerczewski's eagerness to reach Dresden as soon as possible allowed his troops to be spread over a distance of more than 50 kilometers (in an east-west direction) with significant gaps between the various regiments under his command, both Polish and Soviet. This situation was exploited by the 20th Panzer Division together with the 72nd Infantry Division that managed to advance about 6 kilometers inside the Polish lines by counterattacking in a northerly direction from the area south of the town of Diehsa. In this counter-attack, the Germans captured the towns of Diehsa and Kolm, and also reached the vicinity of Spreutz. In addition, the German advance succeeded in cutting the road between Niesky and Bautzen.

For its part, and although further away from the area where the battle for Bautzen took place, the Kampfgruppe of the 545th Division received orders to attack south towards the rear of the 2nd Polish Army during the early morning hours of 21 April. On this day, troops of the German 17th Army were deployed north of Görlitz, having been relieved of their position in the Schenau area.

THE BATTLE OF BAUTZEN

DAY 21. FRIDAY.
During this day the German forces tried to recapture the localities of Weissenberg and Bautzen using their most important units in the sector. The order was that after fighting the Soviet resistance in Weissenberg, a part of the troops used (the men of the "Brandenburg") would immediately go to Bautzen to participate in the attack on the town.
In the early morning hours between the 20th and 21st, the Soviets resumed their attacks in the area of the sawmill and the post office. And once again hand-to-hand fighting between defenders and attackers ensued in all the small pockets of German resistance, the fight was to the death and the Germans knew it well, because up to that moment their fate appeared completely sealed.
On the morning of April 21, Oberst Hoepke, in charge of the city's defense, was again forced to retreat his defensive positions towards the line formed by the Lauengraben-Kornmarkt-Wendischer Grabe-Seidau roads, but at that point the German counterattack to retake Bautzen had begun; in fact, several hours earlier the German pincer attack had begun.
Around 7 or 8 a.m., contacts were established between Hoepke and the Soviets to allow the evacuation of many Germanic wounded who were housed in the Lutheran school building to be secured under Soviet control. Eventually the evacuation took place and the wounded were treated, despite the terrible circumstances that appeared everywhere, correctly and without reprisals, except for the execution of the commander of the 2nd Company of Volkssturm-Bataillone 27/32.
Hoepke also ordered the burning of many buildings, the elementary school and numerous stores, in order to slow down the advance of the combined Soviet armored and infantry forces as much as possible. With all hell breaking loose in the streets of Bautzen, the Germans made good use of the few anti-tank weapons at their disposal: the panzerfaust. But the Soviet advance led by their T-34/85s and IS-2s did not allow the Germans to hold out for long, forcing them to retreat after capturing the main square. Ammunition was scarce and with very few panzerfausts and no heavy artillery, Hoepke's only alternative to stop the Soviet advance was to burn down the entire Seidau district (the fire unintentionally reached the west wing of the castle).
The Germans were forced to retreat to a small pocket of resistance at Ortenburg, west of the city; and optimizing his effort as much as possible, Hoepke ordered small assault groups to attack the Soviets by surprise and immediately undertake the retreat.
Meanwhile, north of Bautzen, the prison was being attacked from two sides by the Soviets. The Volkssturm and prison personnel were tasked to resist these assaults.
The German troops in Bautzen had been reduced to such limited space that they were almost everywhere under the gaze of dangerous Soviet snipers who made it impossible for the troops to move properly through German territory. Here, as Mahé recounts, it was mainly the teenagers of the Hitler Youth who had to face the danger of sniper bullets.
The fighting was becoming increasingly desperate, as the Germans had virtually no positions to retreat to. Every meter of every street was contested by men on both sides, but since the fighting was mainly located in the medieval area of Bautzen, tanks could not be used by the attackers due to the narrowness of the streets in the old town. At this point Hoepke made an announcement to all of his troops urging them to hold each barricade until the end, no matter how small, and ordered his men to resist and prepare for the counterattack rather than be captured by the enemy. Hoepke did not respond to the Soviets' proposed offer of capitulation because, at that moment, he was already in contact with German troops of the General Staff of the 4th Panzer Army who would come to his rescue from the south after telling him, "Hold on, we are coming."

▲ Beautiful current image of the city of Bautzen. Reminiscences of its medieval past can be clearly seen. Public domain by Stephan M. Höhne.

▶ Photograph of Panzertruppen General Fritz-Hübert Gräser, who commanded the 4th Panzer Army and masterfully led it to reorganize after the April 16 attack and subsequently dealt a severe blow to the Soviets and Poles.

▼ Panther tank put out of action by troops of the Polish 2nd Army during the fighting for the city of Bautzen. The losses suffered by the German army were less heavy than those of their enemies, but the Soviet arsenal was almost inexhaustible and the German army was almost totally exhausted at this point in the world conflict. httpwww.kodges.ru.

The Polish troops, as we have commented, were scattered along tens of kilometers like a great "snake"; thus the 7th and 10th Infantry Divisions were still in the "tail" in the line of the Neisse River (engaged in tasks of "cleaning" the Muskauer Forest); in front of these divisions and at a distance of one kilometer were the 16th Polish Armored Brigade and the 5th Infantry Division, and separated by a significant distance in the neck of the snake was the 1st Armored Corps of the Soviet 52nd Army and finally again with a wide gap from the previous unit, at the head of the "snake" approaching the city of Dresden were the 8th and 9th Polish Infantry Divisions. For a better understanding of the existing distances, Bautzen is located about 40 kilometers northeast of Dresden and about 25 kilometers west of Gorlitz. In total, Świerczewski's troops were divided into four groupings that were in full advance with their lines stretched out for 50 kilometers: a perfect target for a final German attack in Saxony.

General Fritz-Hübert Gräser decided that the strong point of the German attack had to be concentrated in the area south of the town of Bautzen, which at that time was the area chosen by General Świerczewski to gather his most delayed troops; although he also deployed his troops to the east and west of his axis of attack as cover for his flanks. Thus he ordered the four divisions belonging to the LVII Panzer-Korps under the command of General der Panzertruppen Kirchner to begin the attack with orders to break the front where the Polish troops were and destroy the maximum number of enemy units that would oppose them. The brunt of the attack would be borne by the two armored units of the LVII Panzer-Korps, while the infantry divisions would take advantage of these actions to outflank the previous ones and create a new defensive line in the eastern part of the attack.

The aforementioned German pincer attack to rescue Bautzen began four hours later with the Panzer-Korps "Grossdeutschland" attacking from the north toward Weissenberg and the LVII Panzer-Korps (commanded by General Kirchner) reinforced with the 17th and 72nd Infantry Divisions attacking from the south toward the north. The objective of this pincer maneuver was to cut off the spearhead of the Polish 2nd Army heading toward Dresden. As we have seen above, the German high command did not miss the opportunity that General Świerczewski's "haste" to advance toward the Saxon capital had created. Immediately, troops under the command of General Fritz-Hübert Gräser, were launched against the formations of the Polish 2nd Army. From positions further to the north, the 500th Armored Engineer Battalion of the "Grossdeutschland", the 2nd Battalion of the 2nd Hunter Regiment of the "Brandenburg" and Kampfgruppe Kappel began their attack against the Polish 2nd Army (in particular against the 5th Infantry Division and some other minor support units). For its part, the Panzer-Korps "Hermann Göring", although weakened, received orders to advance towards the town of Hoyerswerda and launch into combat to close the road to Dresden and advance in an easterly direction.

Thus the enemy would be attacked by German groupings from the east and west at the same time as the attack from the north and south progressed and the German forces met near Mücka (north of Weissenberg) on the morning of April 22.

The 20th Panzer Division, in its broad advance, succeeded in breaking the link between the Soviet 52nd Army and the Polish 2nd Army.

Panzer group general Jauer and the commander of the LVII Panzer Corps (general Kirchner) received orders from the headquarters of the 4th Panzer Army located southwest of Bautzen; in particular, on this 21 April General Jauer of the Panzertruppen had an overview of the recent counterattacks of the 20th Panzer Division and the 1st Parachute Armored Division "Hermann Göring" in the area of Bautzen, while two new counterattacks were ordered with the primary objective of retaking the Soviet-occupied town of Weissenberg. Weissenberg represented a key road junction control point for Soviet troops, as it provided a suitable route for reinforcements and supplies destined for the 52nd Army (which had already been hit and broken up at Kodersdorf by German troops) and also a north-south route suitable for any subsequent Soviet offensive.

Once Weissenberg had been captured by the Germans, it could be used as a foothold to strike back at the Soviets and recapture Bautzen properly. The recapture of Weissenberg was assigned to the Panzer-Grenadier Division "Brandenburg," and once complete its mission would be sent to support the 20th Panzer Division and the 1st Armored Division "Hermann Göring" in their attack on Bautzen.

As mentioned earlier, Weissenberg was captured by the Soviet 7th Guard Mechanized Corps on April 18 and the 294th Rifle Division was left there as a garrison of the town to keep the troop crossing open in an east-west direction allowing the rest of the Mechanized Corps to advance toward Bautzen. But the Soviets did not trust the Germans, especially after the attack of the Panzer-Korps "GD" and the victories at Förstgen and Kodersdorf shortly before, they had warned the 7th Guards Mechanized Corps of the growing danger to the garrison they had deployed at Weissenberg.

But returning to the early hours of the 21st, the German forward movement in the west consisted of the 20th Panzer Division advancing toward Bautzen, while in the east the 17th Infantry Division moved toward Niesky and Weissenberg. Attacking westward at dawn, the 20th Panzer Division and the 300th Tank Brigade reached Soviet defensive positions with anti-tank positions in the area near the highway. After overcoming the anti-tank defense at Gebelzig, the 20th Panzer Division detached one of its battle groups (Kampfgruppe) reinforced by the StuG III of the 300th Tank Brigade that managed to break through the Russian defensive lines on the highway (defended by the 294th Rifle Division) approaching Weissenberg after a hard battle that lasted several hours. With this action, the 20th Panzer Division was able to separate the troops of the Polish 2nd Army (in particular its supply line advancing towards Dresden), from the units of the Soviet 52nd Army (7th Mechanized Corps and the 254th Rifle Division in the area of Bautzen). After defeating the 294th Rifle Division, the German troops moved towards Bautzen, meeting the rear of the 254th Rifle Division, which they would annihilate in a few hours.

Faced with this situation the immediate reaction of the Soviet 52nd Army during that same morning was to order the 25th Guards Mechanized Brigade and the 57th Guards Armored Brigade, positioned south of Bautzen, to move immediately to attack eastward in the direction of Weissenberg to reopen the road after linking up with the 294th Rifle Division following the defeat of this unit by troops of the 20th Panzer Division. But, taking advantage of their powerful attack in that area, the forces of the 20th Panzer Division, led by their armored units, pushed into the deployment area of the fractionated Soviet 52nd Army near Bautzen, causing heavy casualties including the commander of the 73rd Rifle Corps (part of the 254th Infantry Division of the 48th Rifle Corps), General M.K. Puteiko. In their advance, the Germans literally swept the units of the 48th Army Corps and advanced in the direction of Spremberg. Finally, between April 22 and 24, these two units (the 25th Guard Mechanized Brigade and the 57th Guard Armored Brigade) would be surrounded by German units and largely annihilated by troops of the Panzergrenadier Division "Brandenburg". As soon as Weissenberg was recaptured, the now reunified "Brandenburg" Division was sent west for an immediate attack against the Soviets and Poles operating around Bautzen. The bulk of the division maneuvered northwest of the city as a blocking force, while its armored units joined the Wiethersheim battle group to clear Bautzen of Soviet troops. As mentioned above, the offensive action of the LVII Panzer-Korps together with that of the 17th Infantry Division allowed the German forces to meet near Mücka with the Panzer-Korps "Grossdeutschland" (in this case units of the "Brandenburg" Division) on the morning of 22 April. Within a few hours it was possible to deal an important blow to the enemy and to allow a minimal reorganization of the German troops after the attack of the 16th.

The situation in the Bautzen area had changed drastically because thanks to the penetration of the 20th Panzer Division (in the rear of the "Brandenburg" Division), it was possible to establish contact in the Altmark area with the 2nd Hunter Regiment (Jäger-Regiment 2) and the light infantry of the

▲ Image of a column of Wespe self-propelled armored howitzers equipped with 105 guns engaged against the Soviets prior to their penetration into Third Reich territory. Every day the armored force decreased in number, but not in the capacity of its crews. Bundesarchiv.

► A Hummel self-propelled heavy armored howitzer with its massive 150 mm cannon, another of the weapons with which German armored troops faced the Soviets until the end of the war. Bundesarchiv.

▼ Campo della 2a Armata Polacca o Ludowe Wojsko Polskie o LWP al fiume Neisse durante l'aprile 1945. La missione principale di questa unità era di coprire il fianco inferiore del grosso del 1° fronte ucraino. Pubblico dominio.

▲ A Soviet artillery battery bombarding German defensive positions. In this case the target was the Seelow high ground, although in the area of eastern Saxony the Soviet intervention on 16 April was also preceded by heavy artillery fire. Bundesarchiv.

▼ On the left the commander of the 1st Parachute Armored Division "Hermann Göring", Major General Lemke. His bold and courageous command enabled his division to achieve important successes during the fighting in Saxony On the right, Marshal Ivan Koniev in 1945. As commander-in-chief of the 1st Ukrainian Front, he had to quickly solve all the headaches that the intervention of the Polish 2nd Army caused during its advance into eastern Saxony.

"Brandenburg" coming from the Kodersdorf and Ullersdorf area (6 kilometers south of Niesky). This opportunity could not be missed, so immediately von Oppeln-Bronikowski ordered the regiment to advance to recapture the villages of Ullersdorf and Jänkendorf, with the support of Panzerkampfgruppe "Wietersheim" (which was the Sturmgeschütz-Abteilung of the reinforced "Brandenburg" Division, under the command of Captain Walter von Wietersheim). After a stubborn resistance by the Poles of the 7th Infantry Division and the NKFD troops defending both cities, the Germans finally succeeded in the enterprise and both cities were recaptured, although in their state of completely destroyed after these battles.

For its part, the 1st Light Infantry Regiment of the "Brandenburg", deployed further north, was in the vicinity of the 615th z.b.V. (Special Purpose Unit) and left that unit in retreat from the Daubitz and Rietschen area to occupy a new defensive line near Spreefurth.

Meanwhile, at Niesky the men of the two Companies of the "Brandenburg" Engineer Battalion (Panzer-Pionier-Bataillon "Brandenburg") and other German troops under the command of Captain Müller-Rochholz continued the fight to break the encirclement in which they were held. The Soviets began to reinforce their positions with a convoy of trucks captured from the Germans. Meanwhile,

▲ German Field Marshal Ferdinand Schörner, commander-in-chief of Army Group Center, which included the 4th Panzer Army. Despite the state of his troops after the retreat into Reich territory, he managed to create a strong fighting spirit in his troops. Bundesarchiv.

three remaining operational StuG III assault guns were sent to the most critical points in front of the enemy. After advancing about 250 meters, one of these assault guns was able to fire high-powered projectiles directly at the Soviet infantry troops and the trucks in the convoy. Other Soviet attack attempts were stopped before they even began (as in the case of a Cossack cavalry unit). Captain Müller-Rochholz's men found themselves completely surrounded, so the order was given to try to break the encirclement in a westerly direction. The deployment of his troops was led by his three StuG IIIs, which would have had the task of opening the way for a convoy followed by several trucks carrying about 80 wounded. Losses were very high for both the Soviets and the Germans. The breakthrough of the front began at 2:00 a.m. on April 21 after the last shots in the direction of the Russian positions ceased from the German artillery. The Germans reached National Road 115 and destroyed all pockets of Soviet resistance they could find, in some cases with panzerfaust "shots." The "retreat" of Captain Müller-Rochholz's exhausted men was successful, as they were finally able to link up with their comrades from the 20th Panzer Division in the Oedernitz area at dawn the next day.

The 5th Polish Infantry Division under General Aleksander Waszkiewicz and the 16th Armored Brigade, which were positioned further east, were also virtually destroyed in their attempt to counterattack the Germans. These Russian troops received the brutal German assault, initially resisting but always suffering heavy losses. The headquarters of the 5th Infantry Division, guarded only by a few engineer troops and training battalions, unexpectedly came under German attack, leaving numerous losses on the field. In their resistance the men of the Headquarters of the 5th Infantry Division managed to retreat with the help of the 16th Polish Armored Brigade, but they were pursued by the Germans who finally managed to surround them at Förstgen (Forsiegen). Despite the tenacious resistance of the Poles, about 1,300 men, only a little more than a hundred managed to survive (according to Mahé would be about 405 men who managed to escape), losing its commander in chief Aleksander Waszkiewicz. According to some sources, the Polish officer was captured, interrogated, tortured and then executed by German troops.

Even if the surprise was total, the Polish general did not consider the attack of great importance, but a simple "coup de tail" of some German troops still eager to fight (according to some sources, maybe the usual alcohol did not allow Świerczewski to take the right decisions considering the dangerous situation to which his troops had been pushed); so he kept his plan to continue the advance of his vanguard towards Dresden. This new mistake would prove to be definitive in the outcome of the bloody battles that would take place in the following days. But to further increase the operational disaster of the Polish general, due to the German attack, many lines of communication between the different Polish-Soviet units were cut.

The destructive effect of the German attack was so intense that shortly afterwards most of the Polish troops found themselves in absolute chaos, and the already poor cohesion between the various units was further reduced. Suddenly, the troops surrounded by the enemy were now the Polish-Soviets trying to hold out while waiting for support from the rest of the units of the Polish 2nd Army. In these German counterattacks, the 615th Z.b.V. Division managed to establish a stable front line in union with the 17th Infantry Division, which was beginning to deploy to the area that had held the "Hermann Göring". Thanks to the advance of these units, small German groups that had remained behind the Soviet-Polish lines in their dazzling advance, such as those still holding out in the Muskauer Forest, joined German troops advancing into territory previously occupied by the Poles. The Panzer-Korps "Grossdeutschland" also finally managed to escape its third encirclement since the beginning of the Neisse crossing by the Soviets and the Poles, managing to rejoin the bulk of the 4th Panzer Army, although not all the Germans who had remained behind enemy lines were so lucky. Thus in the village of Niederkaina (in the vicinity of Bautzen in 1945, and today a district of the city) an undetermined number of members of Volkssturm-Bataillone 27/32 (at least the 120 mentioned above, although some sources raise the figure to 254, as in the case of Mahé) who had been captured by Polish-Soviet troops, were locked up in a barn which was then set on fire. This action, a real war crime, took place in full retreat after the German attack and was largely motivated by the state of panic in which Polish troops were before the violent German attack against the Polish 2nd Army. Almost all of the prisoners died in the barn fire; only two men managed to escape.

DAY 22. SATURDAY

As we commented in the events of the previous day, the men of the engineer battalion commanded by Captain Müller-Rochholz managed to reach the town of Oedernitz at dawn. However, they had to struggle until the very last moment, because before they could link up with the men of the 20th Panzer Division, they had to get rid of a Russian battery with their StuG III assault guns. Later, Müller-Rochholz's StuG IIIs reached the positions of the 20th Panzer Division. In these attacks important successes were achieved as more than 50 tanks and 100 enemy vehicles were destroyed, in addition to much captured material including food and gasoline.

It should be remembered that at dawn on the 22nd the 20th Panzer Division had managed to contact units of the "Brandenbeurg" Division near Mücka, thus they had managed to definitively break the line held by the Poles and Soviets. In the headquarters of the Polish 2nd Army urgent decisions began to be made to try to solve the serious danger that hour after hour was threatening the integrity of Polish units. Thus, despite his initial reluctance to stop the advance towards Dresden, General Świerczewski was finally forced to change his initial idea ordering to stop the advance and immediately retrace his

▲ Finally, the Soviet advance through southern Germany made it possible to link up with American troops on the Elbe River near Torgau. But German troops continued to make the Soviet advance through Saxony difficult. Public Domain

▶ Emblem used by units of the elite Red Army Guard. Many of these units were involved in the fighting for Eastern Saxony. Public Domain

▼ An ISU-152 World War II veteran rests in the Muzeum Polskiej Techniki Wojskowej in Warsaw. The Polish eagle emblem is clearly visible on the side of the vehicle. Public domain from SuperTank17.

▲ T-34/85 tanks of the Polish 2nd Army advance along a German road in 1945. The impressive German infrastructure of roads and highways greatly aided the speed of the Red Army's advance into the Reich. Public Domain

▼ Left Photograph of the veteran commander-in-chief of the 20th Panzer Division during the fighting for Eastern Saxony, Major General Hermann von Oppeln-Bronikowski. Bundesarchiv. Right Emblem of the 10th SS Panzer Division "Frundsberg". Only 200 men took part in the fighting for Bautzen, as they were left behind the bulk of their unit when they were sent north in the midst of the Soviet assault on the Oder-Neisse line.

steps in order to prevent the gap created by the Germans near Bautzen from increasing and endangering the southern flank of the bulk of the 1st Ukrainian Front.

Immediately, the 1st Armored Corps shifted its advance in the direction of Dresden to the rear to support the troops attacked by the Germans in the central area of the offensive line of the 2nd Polish Army where the 5th Infantry Division was overwhelmed. The 8th Infantry Division was also ordered back on its heels, as was the 1st Armored Corps, with the task of closing the gap the Germans had created in their line of advance. These units, which were to hold back the Germans, encountered numerous Polish soldiers fleeing their disastrous defeat. As Mahé quotes, "General Świerczewski's contradictory orders contributed to the chaos at a time when his troops needed instead to regain confidence and cohesion." Despite everything, General Świerczewski did not consider it necessary to withdraw the 9th Polish Infantry Division, which kept its orders to advance towards the vicinity of Dresden. General Świerczewski's orders were becoming decisive in the face of the disastrous Polish-Soviet advance; to this it must be added that, after the beginning of the German offensive, General Świerczewski lost direct communication with his superiors of the 1st Ukrainian Front and therefore with Marshal Koniev. In the absence of news from the Polish 2nd Army, Marshal Koniev sent his chief of staff General Ivan Yefimovich Petrov and his chief of operations General Vladimir Ivanovich Kostylev to inform him urgently of the situation on his southern flank. After Koniev's two emissaries had contacted the Polish general, communications with the High Command of the 1st Belorussian Front were re-established and General Petrov temporarily dismissed General Świerczewski for his unacceptable errors in the conduct of the advance, being replaced by General Kostylev. Immediately, Marshal Koniev, faced with the gravity of the situation, ordered that the 14th and 95th Guard Rifle Divisions and the 4th Guard Armored Corps, along with five other units, be sent to the area to reinforce the battered Poles. These units "broke away" from the 1st Ukrainian Front and began their advance toward Kamenz, Königswartha, and Sdier, with the intention of slowing the possible advance of the victorious German troops farther north. Koniev was not willing to allow the German advance, so he increased the air support for the Polish and Soviet troops in the area of Bautzen. We must not forget that already almost at the end of the war the dominance of the skies belonged almost exclusively to the Soviet Air Force, countered only on a few occasions by small formations of Luftwaffe aircraft. As for the planes that supported the powerful army with which the Poles and Soviets faced the Germans, these belonged to the 2nd Air Army, assigned to this area to support the ground troops. This 2nd Air Army was based in the 3rd Air Assault Corps, the 2nd Air Fighter Corps, part of the 4th Air Bombardment Corps, and the 6th Guards Bombardment Corps, which had been assigned exclusively to support the Polish 2nd Army and the 52nd Army.

As Marshal Koniev "moved" his pieces to stop the enemies, German troops advanced southeast of the city of Bautzen, eliminating the Polish troops. Among the Soviet-Polish troops, some remained trapped behind the German front line, including the 294th Soviet Rifle Division, which was eventually surrounded at Weissenberg by troops of the "Brandenburg" Division.

Also in the early hours of the 22nd, Korchagine received a radio message from the 52nd Army informing him of Koniev's decision to withdraw from Bautzen the two Soviet units that were engaged in the fighting (the 25th Guards Mechanized Brigade and the 57th Guards Armored Brigade belonging to the 7th Guards Mechanized Corps) to use them in a counterattack against Diehsa. These two units should theoretically have been united with the Polish 1st Armored Corps to begin the counter-attack at 13.00 hours by the three units together. In the meantime, between 09.00 and 10.00 the 25th Guard Mechanized Brigade and the 57th Guard Armored Brigade (which had been reinforced for this attack with 2000 men, 15 tanks, 17 armored vehicles and 36 howitzers and mortars) began their attack in the direction of Weissenberg.

Shortly after receiving Koniev's orders, at noon on April 22 Korchagine ordered his attack in the direction of Bautzen to be halted and directed the 57th Armored Brigade of Guards and the 25th Mechanized Brigade with a total of 2043 men, 15 tanks, 17 self-propelled vehicles, 26 guns, and nine armored vehicles to retrace their steps in an easterly direction to reach Weissenberg; in command of these troops he sent Major General Maximov. Once the lines of the 294th Rifle Division were reached, Maximov would take command of the city's defense. Reserve troops of the 7th Polish Infantry Division would also arrive from the north.

At the same time, the Polish 1st Armored Corps, which had retraced its steps after the order to "close" the gap created by the Germans, received the aforementioned order to attack together with the Soviet troops of the Guard from the area north of Bautzen through Baruth toward Gross Radish. The intention was to wipe out all German resistance in the Diehsa and Kolm area. However, inadequate communications between the various attacking units caused the Soviet troops to move exclusively north of Bautzen to meet up with the 1st Armored Corps without proceeding to Gross Radish.

For the German attack on Weissenberg, the 2nd Battalion of the 2nd Fighter Regiment of the Panzer-Grenadier Division "Brandenburg" and also the 2nd Battalion of the 1st Fighter Regiment of "Brandenburg" arrived. The movements took place on 23 April in the area of the left wing of the 4th Panzer Army with very clear orders: the capture of Gröditz, northwest of Weissenberg following the course of the Löbauer Wasser river. During the advance, the German troops encountered some Polish units of the 7th Polish Infantry Division that they had to repel. The 2nd Battalion of the 1st Hunter Regiment of the "Brandenburg" and the 1st Battalion (gep) of the "Brandenburg" were unified and together with them also the assault tank unit of the "Brandenburg" was deployed and assembled in Gröditz. These troops prepared to support the rest of the 1st Hunter Regiment in their attack which was to occur shortly. While the two hunter regiments, the 1st and 2nd, advanced toward Weissenberg, the Armored Engineer Assault Battalion "Brandenburg" remained in reserve for reinforcements. On April 23, the Engineers moved westward into the area south of Bautzen. On April 24, the 2nd Fighter Regiment prepared for combat; then the 1st Battalion of the 2nd Fighter Regiment led the attack toward Weissenberg supported by the troops of the 2nd Battalion. The Soviets, who had been warned of the approach of the "Brandenburg" troops, did not prepare a solid defense. In fact, while German forces were expected from the south and even from the east, the "Brandenburg" troops of the 2nd Battalion appeared from the north, which was a great surprise to the defenders. Soviet troops in Weissenberg were short of fuel, ammunition and food, so General Maximov considered it wise not to get surrounded. So he ordered his infantry and armored troops to exit the city through what he considered a gap in the German defensive lines to the northeast in order to flee east toward Diehsa; but as we will see later this attempt proved to be completely unsuccessful because the Germans had already completed their encirclement. Faced with significant damage across the entire front line, the 26th Guards Mechanized Brigade, which had participated in the bloody fighting in the town of Bautzen, was ordered to withdraw and take defensive positions between Burk and Pliesskowitz.

At the end of the 22nd the situation was still favorable to the Germans, who were making good progress in their advance towards Lohsa, Hoyerswerda and Spremberg. A large part of the Polish 2nd Army was practically at a standstill and the units that tried to stop the Germans threw themselves directly "towards the precipice". On the Polish side, the chaos was total as the Germans had managed to split the Polish 2nd Army into 4 different groups completely cut off from each other; and other units were also suffering a very high number of losses, such as the Polish 5th Division and the Polish 16th Armored Brigade, which had been virtually annihilated, both units losing nearly 90% of their personnel.

As German troops tried to recapture Bautzen, the garrison troops commanded by Hoepke continued to resist. But knowing that their comrades were trying to liberate them, and also thanks to some supplies they had received in the early dark hours of the morning of April 22 thanks to a Luftwaffe plane (other attempts to resupply ammunition failed due to bad weather), allowed them to keep their morale up to continue the relentless fight.

DAY 23. SUNDAY

During the night of April 22-23, they regrouped southeast of Bautzen to again attempt to strike the line of junction between the Polish 2nd Army and the 52nd Army.

The German advance continued, reaching the Schwarzer Schöps River to the east and the towns of Lohsa, Grossdubrau, and Oppitz to the west of their line of attack. The bulk of the German troops positioned themselves in the wooded area around Lohsa, while their vanguard moved toward Königswartha and Hoyerswerda.

In the city, Hoepke continued to reject any attempt of surrender by his men, in fact it was decreed that any man who abandoned his position would be sentenced to death and executed. Shortly afterwards one of the few Luftwaffe attacks from the air on Soviet positions inside the city took place, a fact that managed to raise a little the morale of the defenders.

During the morning of 23 April, the 1st Parachute Armored Division "Hermann Göring", which had reorganized in Kodersdorf during these first days of the German attack, moved in the direction of Bautzen from the south and southeast. Near Hochkirch a fierce battle took place between Panther tanks of the Panzer Regiment of the 1st Parachute Armored Division "Hermann Göring" advancing in the direction of Highway 6 and several enemy T-34s. In this battle many Soviet tanks were destroyed. In the evening the 1st Parachute Armoured Division "Hermann Göring" (attacking south-east of Cunewalde) once reinforced with the 311th Tank Brigade, together with the 20th Panzer Division (led by Combat Group Wiethersheim) and the 300th Tank Brigade, entered the city of Bautzen from the east and southeast (other units such as the Assault Engineers of the "Brandenburg" or troops of the 1st Hunter Regiment of the same unit also participated). At that time the area held by the German defenders stationed in the location besieged by the Polish-Soviets was no wider than 150 m2. The German attacking force included about 40 armored vehicles, including tanks and assault tanks (including some jagdpanzers).

The Panther tanks of the Panzer Regiment of the 1st Parachute Armored Division "Hermann Göring" took Wuischke, Pielitz and Binnewitz, arriving around 3:00 p.m. on the Goldenen Höhe at Rabitz; after observing, from this hill, the waiting Soviet troops, they managed to destroy 8-10 Soviet anti-tank guns with their tanks. From the hill, Rossmann's Panthers advanced towards the "hussar barracks" and succeeded in freeing the western part of the building from the enemy after knocking down part of the walls after a fight that lasted 2-3 hours. Oberstleutnant Rossmann demonstrated once again in these days his great skills as commander of armored units, as he had already demonstrated previously in East Prussia after serving initially in the 16th anti-aircraft artillery battery of the "Hermann Göring" Division.

Meanwhile, the 20th Panzer Division for its part was attacking from the northeast of the city and was recovering the villages of Kreckwitz and Burk from the hands of Soviets who were increasingly frightened to see the powerful attack organized by an army they considered only a few days earlier as little less than defeated.

To try to make clearer to the reader the German device to reconquer Bautzen, we make a small summary of it: attacking from the west was the bulk of the German infantry supported by armored elements of the 20th Panzer Division; on the left flank of that Division, and attacking from the northwest (between Falkenberg and Auritz), was the bulk of the Parachute Armored Division "Hermann Göring 1"; Advancing north of the town in search of Highway 96 were the "Wiethersheim" battle group and the men of the 2nd regiment of the 1st Parachute Armored Division "Hermann Göring" (these two formations were joined in the evening of the same day by troops of the Panzer-Grenadier Division "Brandenburg" from Weissenberg).

Once they reach the city, German troops enter the streets in large numbers. The fighting with the Soviet troops turns into a real bloodbath, again street by street, building by building and room by room.

▲ Although less powerful than the ISU.152, the SU-85s were the perfect complement to them. Here we observe a veteran Polish SU-85 Muzeum Polskiej Techniki Wojskowej in Warsaw. Public Domain by SuperTank17.

▼ Left: The Polish Lieutenant General Karol Świerczewski, who after the World War was considered thanks to Soviet propaganda a hero and a great strategist despite being a real failure. On the right is Major General Hermann Schulte-Heuthaus, commander-in-chief of the Panzer-Grenadier Division "Brandenburg". His performance in command of his unit was decisive, as he was able to regroup it after it had been split into several parts following the attack of the 1st Ukrainian Front across the Neisee River. Public Domain

Once again the brewery will witness bloody struggles for control, the difference being that now it was the Soviets who were worse off. As the Germans advanced, small reserves were being left behind where the Soviets were reinforcing a foothold. The Reichenturm (a 15th century tower) returns to German hands. Nazi troops approach Muskauer Street, where they are momentarily stopped by fierce resistance. The advance of the "Hermann Göring" troops (mainly Panzer grenadiers of the 2nd regiment of the 1st Parachute Armored Division "Hermann Göring"), with the support of the men of the 20th Panzer Division, continued to take the Schützenplatz and subsequently surrounded a good number of enemy troops in Ortenburg who in turn had encircled a group of German troops from the city's garrison (men of the 7th Company of the 2nd Regiment of the 1st Parachute Armored Division "Hermann Göring" also managed to create a small bridgehead on the west bank of the Spree and capture the railroad bridge intact, allowing the armored troops of the 300th Tank Brigade to enter the city). These German troops were able to contact the small "Frundsberg" battle group (which had previously been evacuated from the city and was blocking the area against possible Soviet incursions) positioned on the outskirts of the city.

Faced with the uncontested German advance, Korchagine ordered the 24th Guard Mechanized Brigade, which was inside the city, to urgently go to the German advance zone in Bautzen. But the situation turns out to be much worse than Korchagine thought, as the 24th Guards Mechanized Brigade could not go anywhere, since the advancing panzer-grenadiers of the 2nd Regiment of the 1st Parachute Armored Division "Hermann Göring" even reached the area where the unit's General Staff is located (in the town hall) and surrounded it. At 17:00 the German panzer-grenadiers supported by some armored vehicles managed to break through the Soviet defensive lines that protected the barracks-base of military training of the Hussars, reconquering it.

The situation became more and more critical for the Soviets who eventually had to flee to the north of the city, also having to give up the siege to the survivors of the Bautzen garrison at Ortenburg (in their retreat the men of the 7th Mechanized Guard Corps received orders to rejoin the 4th Armored Guard Corps). The Germans who had resisted the Soviet assault led by Hoepke for several days had succeeded in accomplishing their mission of "fixing" as long as possible (4 days of tenacious and well-trained resistance by their commander-in-chief that allowed the second level units to hold off elite armored troops like those used by the Soviets at Bautzen) the maximum number of enemy units while waiting for a German response. A response that had become reality thanks to the troops of the 1st Armored Parachute Division "Hermann Göring" and the 20th Panzer Division, who were very negatively surprised when they could verify that a large part of the population had not been evacuated before the fighting, often ending up as victims of the friendly fire of the "rescuers" (the troops of the "Hermann Göring who did not know that many civilians were still in the city, had begun to use incendiary bullets but after knowing the fact always ascertained their targets before firing).

Step by step the Panzergrenadiers of the 2nd Regiment of the 1st Armored Parachute Division "Hermann Göring" recaptured the city, testifying that the Soviets, in their escape, had burned the food depot they had in the city. In many cases, accounts agree that many of the Soviet troops were fighting drunk because they had taken over some of the city's liquor stores. A final attempt at a Soviet attack inside Bautzen supported by at least 20 T-34/85s and assault guns was crushed by the highly motivated Germans who were determined to completely take the city.

For their part the Soviet-Polish, seeing that Bautzen was completely lost, tried to hold back the German troops in the area near Bautzen to avoid further disaster. Thus they placed the 73rd Army Corps (of the 52nd Army), the 1st Armored Corps, and the 254th Rifle Division back to block the possible German advance route. At the foot of the western hills of Bautzen, for their part, troops of the 20th Panzer Division and the 1st Armored Parachute Division "Hermann Göring" struck the defensive positions of the 254th Rifle Division and continued to advance.

Also outside the city, the German troops went on the offensive trying to make the most of the critical state of their enemies after the fall of Bautzen; the objective in these final moments of the war was clear: destroy as many retreating enemy units as possible.

So the main German units went on the attack. The Fallschirm-Panzer-Korps "Hermann Göring" (General Staff) reached the north of Bautzen and began its offensive in the direction of Lohsa-Oppitz-Grossdubrau, being supported by the 615th Division z.b.V. In their advance they succeeded in pushing back the Poles in the embankment of the Schwarzer Schöps, and approached the vanguard of the 7th Mechanized Guard Corps, which they tried to encircle.

Further east, in the area of Weissenberg, the German advance also obtained important successes thanks to the men of the Panzer-Grenadier Division "Brandenburg". In the area the Germans succeeded in repelling the attacks of the 5th and 57th Guards Brigades, inflicting severe damage, as about 50 tanks and 100 Soviet vehicles of all types were destroyed.

At the same time, the 1st "Brandenburg" Infantry Regiment captured Gröditz, west of Bautzen, which allowed it to completely encircle General Maximov's 294th Rifle Division, which had remained behind enemy lines due to the lightning German advance. Attempts by the 5th and 57th Guards Brigade to free their comrades of the 294th Rifle Division were resolutely repulsed by the Germans.

In the meantime, while the advance continued, German troops were detached to annihilate this "pocket" as well; although to a lesser extent the same fate befell other small pockets of Soviet groups that were "eliminated" by the Germans.

The result of the fighting to recapture Weissenberg was that the 294th Rifle Division, the 57th Armored Brigade of the Guards and the 25th Mechanized Brigade of the Guards were annihilated by the attacks of the "Brandenburg". It was an incredible victory for this division in this final phase of the war, considering that the "Brandenburg" had to act in separate groups because they had not yet been regrouped. Maximov's last orders were for his troops to try to reach the Soviet lines of the 52nd Army in an easterly direction. Many of these men who tried to escape in small groups were captured or shot; and even some groups of Soviets ended up in the defense zone of the German 17th Army and annihilated on April 25.

The Polish 7th Infantry Division and its artillery and anti-tank groupings of the Polish 2nd Army that had been operating northeast of Weissenberg were also overwhelmed by the German counterattack, despite the desperate defense put up by the Polish artillery, as their units quickly lost cohesion and ended up routed by the German counterattack. At least 3000 Soviets and Poles were killed in this battle, with an unknown number of prisoners. One of the captured prisoners was Maximov who was seriously wounded by a German rocket.

The total number of German armored vehicles that tried to collapse the front held by the Polish-Soviets in the area near the town of Bautzen reached more than 100 tanks, assault guns and tank destroyers that day. In spite of the difficulties, the Luftwaffe also contributed in its own small way against a numerically far superior enemy in the Saxon skies.

Despite the German successes, it still remained clear that the front had not been broken through the positions of the 73rd Rifle Corps of the 52nd Army on the Görlitz-Richen axis, which prevented the rear of the Polish units of the 2nd Army from fully reaching the front.

While the battle for Bautzen seemed to be decided in favor of the Germans, the troops of the Polish 2nd Army continued their advance with the 5th, 8th, and 9th Infantry Divisions, advancing about 18 kilometers by the end of the day. At that point, after reaching the Kamenz-Seifensdorf line, they began to confront the troops of the newly arrived 2nd Parachute Grenadier Division "Hermann Göring".

For their part, the 10th and 7th Polish Infantry Divisions resisted the German assault as best they could in the woods south of the Weisswasser-Kreba-Stochteich line. By the end of the day, the German troops had succeeded after five days of heavy fighting in breaking through the enemy troop front and advancing about 20 kilometers in a northerly direction to the area south of the town of Klitten.

DAY 24. MONDAY

The German vanguards still managed to make progress against the increasingly reinforced enemy troops, highlighting the possibility of finally "breaking" the southern flank of the 1st Ukrainian Front. The German troops also had a second problem, impossible to solve at that moment, and that would have proved definitive in the evolution of the fighting: the extreme lack of fuel to be able to carry out their plans. The final result was the order to slow down the advance of the troops towards the north. But in the meantime, despite the fact that the offensive was slowing down, the Germans were determined to eliminate the enemy troops that were trapped between their lines.

And of course, the "pocket" in which the Soviet 294th Rifle Division had been trapped was tightening by the minute. As noted above, Maximov ordered the evacuation of the pocket where his troops were encircled, but this order was taken without his knowledge that the 4th Panzer Army had already established a continuous front to the east, making any attempt by Weissenberg's troops to reach the 52nd Army quite unlikely. So Maximov devised a plan to try to escape the encirclement, and at 06:00 on the 24th he began this Soviet attempt by following the two roads leading to Gebelzig. But the desperation of the Soviet soldiers in trying to escape annihilation by the Germans caused numerous snags that eventually caused the Germans to notice and act against this escape attempt. As the two columns of Soviets moved northeast from Weissenberg along open fields Major General Hermann Schulte-Heuthaus, commander of the "Brandenburg" determined to prevent this, ordered heavy artillery fire against the Soviets while sending infantry units including Volkssturm Battalion 21/128 or the 464th Division (which had established a defensive cordon northeast of Weissenberg). After the artillery attack, in which rockets were also used, numerous Soviet tanks and vehicles were destroyed. It was the troops of the 1st and 2nd battalions that carried out a joint attack later supported by the assault guns of the "Brandenburg" accompanying the 1st Fighter Regiment. At 14:30 the German troops regrouped in the area of the Wuischker factory and reached the entire section of the railway line west of Weissenberg. The German pressure completely prevented the Soviet escape attempt, so the survivors of the Soviet 294th Rifle Division had to retreat into the forest northeast of Weissenberg. Without any respite the German troops harassed the retreat of the Soviet troops who were virtually pinned down, leaving them the only option of attempting to return to Weissenberg where they were eventually trapped again, in this case by troops of the German 17th Infantry Division who "appeared" from Niederseifersdorf after creating a secure front line at Weisse Schöps. Only a few men and vehicles of the Soviet unit managed to escape from the encirclement into the forest, despite directions issued by their commander Maximov. The result was great carnage, as every Soviet attempt to escape was everywhere stifled and crushed by the Germans. Many of the Soviets also abandoned their equipment trying to escape, with mixed luck. Finally, once the Soviet 294th Rifle Division was completely annihilated, some prisoners were taken, most notably its commander, who had been wounded by a grenade and had to be sent to the Zittau POW camp, where both of his legs were amputated. Later, during the Soviet offensive for Prague, he was freed, but he died in May for the serious wounds suffered.

In the "pocket" of the 294th Rifle Division, the Germans managed to capture numerous Soviet war materials, including many American-made trucks from the loan agreement between the United States and the U.S.S.R. (at least 1,500 vehicles of all types). In addition, the Germans counted at least 3,000 Russian soldiers killed, which shows the dramatic scope that combat had for the Soviets. For their part, the men of the "Brandenburg" suffered 216 casualties, including 57 killed. Ultimately, the battle for the "pocket" of Weissenberg, completely eliminated the Soviet 294th Rifle Division from the Red

▲ View of an ISU-152 at Kubinka. This vehicle fulfilled the dual role of a self-propelled gun and tank destroyer and proved to be a great enemy for German panzers. Public Domain by Saiga20K.

► The Polish eagle called "Orzel Bialy" was and is the coat of arms of Poland and was usually depicted on its armored vehicles as a plain white eagle or as a white eagle with a red background. Public Domain

▼ Two T-34/85s belonging to the Polish 4th Armored Brigade of the Polish 1st Armored Corps. On the side of both towers is the "Orzel Bialy" or Polish eagle. Public Domain

Army's order of battle.

Thus, once the majority of the encircled Soviet 294th Rifle Division had been annihilated at Weissenberg, the Germans were able to prevent any Polish and Soviet military operations in the eastern part of the Soviet advance, which served to prepare the subsequent German attack towards Bautzen to conclude the final capture of that city. This victory was complete. In fact, on the night of the 23rd to the 24th, the men of the 7th Company of Fallschirmjäger-Panzer Regiment 2 established a bridgehead over the Spree, allowing the armored units of the 300th Tank Brigade to reach the railway viaduct on the west bank. As soon as Weissenberg was recaptured, the first units of the "Brandenburg" division were sent west for an immediate attack against the Soviets and Poles operating around Bautzen (as mentioned above, the first of these units, including its armored troops, joined the Wiethersheim battle group to liberate Bautzen from incoming Soviet troops on the evening of the 23rd). For its part, the bulk of the division maneuvered northwest of the city as a blocking force.

In particular, the final capture of Bautzen was conducted by the 20th Panzer Division on the morning of April 24. In the early hours of the day, the combat group of the 20th Panzer Division, accompanied by Schwere Panzerjäger Abteilung 88, was in Purschwitz, only 7 kilometers from Bautzen, and was advancing toward it. But the Soviets were waiting for them and ambushed the Germans at the Purschwitz road bridge. The German advance seemed to be stalled, but thanks to the artillery of the 20th Panzer Division and especially one of the increasingly rare Luftwaffe ground attack missions, it was possible to continue the advance. Once again the Stukas of Schlacht-Geschwader 2 supported their comrades despite the absolute aerial dominance of the Soviets. When the advance continued, the troops of the 20th Panzer Division suffered an air raid, which in this case was unfortunately "friendly fire", as a Focke Wulf Fw 190 mistook them for Soviet troops advancing on Bautzen. Again the advance was resumed and when they passed through Niederkaina, they discovered with astonishment and horror the massacre committed by the Poles against the German prisoners they had locked up in the aforementioned farm. The fight was very bloody, but after learning the behavior of the enemy towards the prisoners, the troops decided that no man would be captured, the fight would be to the death. The armored unit reached Kreckwitz and then executed an attack on Basankwitz where soldiers of the Soviet 254th Rifle Division confronted them.

After several days of fighting, contact was finally made with the two small German groups that were still holding out against the Polish-Soviets, as they had almost captured the town. About 400 men had fiercely resisted the countless enemy attacks. The commander-in-chief of the 20th Panzer Division, Hermann von Oppeln-Bronikowski was able to coordinate his attack from the south of the city with the German troops trapped in Bautzen, which in turn enabled this latest German triumph. In particular, a German patrol was sent to Ortenburg to contact the defenders shortly before the men of the "Hermann Göring" reached the area after some very bloody battles in which street by street, house by house and room by room fighting was repeated, even using the sewers to gain access to the stronghold where the defenders of Bautzen still held out. The Polish-Soviet troops tried to hold their positions with fierce resistance, as they expected support from the rest of the Polish troops further north, although this never happened.

The "rescue" of the defenders of Ortenburg finally took place around 10:00 a.m., when finally the Hitler Youth, sent by Hoepke to contact the German troops coming to their rescue, ran into the German armored vanguard. Although von Oppeln-Bronikowski expected to find at least about 1,200 defenders, he was surprised to find only about 400 completely exhausted.

Korchagin, seeing himself in such a compromising situation, sent the reserve of the 24th Mechanized Brigade consisting of 3 T-34/85s, 3 anti-aircraft guns and a reconnaissance company to try to block the access of German troops to rescue the besieged to Ortenburg Castle. In addition, Korchagin ordered

▲ Remains of the battle that took place in the so-called "valley of death" in the area of Panschwitz-Kuckau and Crostwitz, where the 9th Polish Infantry Division was ambushed and practically annihilated.

▲ An SU-85 self-propelled cannon belonging to the 13th Self-Propelled Artillery Regiment. Although smaller in caliber than other Soviet tank destroyers, it was considered fearsome by German panzers.

▼ Impressive close-up of the very powerful Soviet IS-2 at Kubinka. This tank was used not only by the Soviets in the fighting in Lusatia (Eastern Saxony) but also by the Poles. Public Domain by Saiga20K.

the staff of the 24th mechanized brigade to hold the town hall and then ordered them to retreat to the northern suburbs to avoid being surrounded (all this despite Marshal Koniev's orders clearly stating that the town could never be surrendered and had to be defended to the end).

With great euphoria, the German troops, once they had freed the defenders, tried to avoid the withdrawal of enemy troops from Bautzen to the north, as we have already mentioned. And although the Germans were able to hit the rear of the fleeing troops, they also suffered losses, such as the 26 men of a Volkssturm unit who were ambushed while trying to "hunt down" one of the retreating enemy units. These Volkssturm men were captured only to be shot in the back of the head shortly thereafter in a barn near Burk, as Mahé recounts.

The recapture of Bautzen can be considered the last great tactical success of German troops in the world conflict, since the city after these events remained in German hands until the surrender of the Reich. Although it is true that in the two weeks of war that still remained, German troops achieved occasional successes against the Soviets mainly and always with the intention of gaining time to be able to withdraw both civilians and troops to the west preferring by far to be captured by the Western Allies and thus trying to avoid captivity with the Soviets.

Immediately after achieving the goal of taking Bautzen and saving the last remaining defenders, von Oppeln-Bronikowski began to reorganize his troops, as well as those who had so bravely resisted the enemy under Hoepke's command. In particular, and in order not to underutilize his already scarce manpower, he reviewed the various summary death sentences that some of the defenders of Bautzen had received and commuted them to an obligation of continued participation in the fighting to come, since any man capable of wielding a weapon was at that time needed. In fact, it was the defenders of Bautzen who were tasked by von Oppeln-Bronikowski to wipe out the small pockets of enemy resistance that remained within the city (supported by Stukas and weapons supplied by von Oppeln-Bronikowski's troops), while his veteran units would be tasked with holding off enemy attempts to recapture Bautzen.

Thus, even though the town was recaptured by the Germans, as the commander in chief of the 20th Panzer Division had predicted, enemy counterattacks immediately began from the north. Faced with the loss of the city, the Soviet high command tried to remedy the situation by sending several units to recover the city. Among these units, the 8th Infantry Division, which was to be united with the 7th and 10th Infantry Divisions or the 1st Armored Corps (which regrouped at dusk between Burk and Malschwitz) stands out. In all cases, the Polish-Soviet troops failed to break the defending German forces.

In fact, at dusk on the 24th and in the early hours of the 25th a new attempt was made by the Polish 1st Armored Corps (and in particular by the Polish 2nd Armored Brigade) along Highway 6 to reach Stiebitz. From there it launched a counterattack west of the town of Bautzen. The Poles started from the road west of Bautzen, unloading their attack against the German defensive lines held by the 2nd Regiment of the 1st Parachute Armored Division "Hermann Göring" (II./ Fallschirm-Panzer-Grenadier Regiment 1) and supported by men of Combat Group "Frundsberg" and armored vehicles belonging to the 300th Tank Brigade. Since the Germans had no anti-tank weapons to face the Polish armored vehicles, the situation became very dangerous for them, but the Polish 1st Armored Corps had been too hasty in conducting its attacks based on its armored vehicles with minimal infantry or artillery support. Thanks to this situation, the Germans were able to stop the attack and later forced the Poles to retreat to their starting positions (in the area of Salzenforst and Bolbritz) thanks to the attack on the flank of the Polish 2nd Armored Brigade of "Hermann Göring" troops. In this battle, the German troops led by the 1st Parachute Armored Division "Hermann Göring" inflicted a hard blow to the 2nd Polish Armored Brigade, destroying 17 tanks, 120 wounded and 42 dead.

After the soldiers of the 1st Armored Parachute Division "Hermann Göring" managed to stop the Polish counterattacks that attempted to recapture Bautzen, the soldiers of the 2nd Polish Army "trapped" in the Saxon city continued to resist in smaller and smaller pockets that became nests of resistance until they were finally defeated in the following days mainly by the men of the garrison of Bautzen. While the fighting continued for the city, the Soviet air force carried out numerous attacks against the Germans, although they did not bear the hoped-for fruit of breaking the unstoppable German avalanche against the Poles and Soviets.

Among many troop movements on both sides in the Bautzen area of operations, there was one that proved crucial for the Germans. A reconnaissance unit of the "Hermann Göring" Division, which was reorganizing at Bloaschütz, surprised and neutralized a part of the General Staff of the Polish 2nd Army. In the corpse of one of the Poles they found some documents with plans for the retreat of the 9th Polish Infantry Division from the Dresden area to the positions of the Polish 2nd Army. This allowed the Germans to inflict the maximum possible punishment on the Polish unit only a few days later.

Despite the German success, the grenadiers of the 1st Armored Parachute Division "Hermann Göring" had suffered heavy losses. During the afternoon the 24th Guards Armored Brigade finally withdrew north of Bautzen. The immediate order of the 1st Ukrainian Front was clear, Bautzen was to be recaptured immediately. That same afternoon, troops of the 1st Armored Parachute Division "Hermann Göring" were deployed west of the town of Bautzen, in the area of the highway to Dresden near Sanzenforst and Boaschütz. While Lemke's men would prevent further attempts to free their comrades trapped in Bautzen, Wiethersheim's battle group remained inside the town to break up pockets of enemy resistance. These mostly encircled Soviet soldiers were prepared to fight to the end, and in some cases where soldiers surrendered it was not uncommon for them to be immediately executed following the no-prisoners rule, given the brutality with which they themselves had behaved towards civilians and defenders of the Bautzen garrison (though not in all cases).

Meanwhile, the 933rd Rifle Regiment of the 294th Rifle Brigade, which was trying to retreat in the direction of Schafberg, was reinforced by 27 assault tanks belonging to a Polish regiment. But once again the few Stukas that SG 2 could put in the air made their appearance, destroying 4 SU-76 and forcing the enemy to flee in a disorderly fashion.

Major General von Oppeln-Bronikowski, taking advantage of the tactical situation and the disposition of the German troops and those of his adversaries, decided to take the maximum advantage. Thus, the Armored Parachute Division 1 "Hermann Göring", whose headquarters were located in Löbau, was ordered to protect the southern flank of the 20th Panzer Division and to reintegrate the Panzer Regiment of "Hermann Göring" (Fallschirmjäger-Panzer Regiment 1) under the command of Oberstleutnant Rossman into its unit. The Panzer Regiment would receive new orders confirming the German intention to advance northward, specifically to Hoyerswerda, only 30 kilometers northwest of Bautzen.

DAY 25. TUESDAY

During this day in the interior of Bautzen the fighting continued against the dwindling pockets of Soviet resistance. There was no mercy, as demonstrated by the men of the Wiethersheim Combat Group when in the northern quarter of the city they captured and later executed some wounded and medical personnel of the 254th Rifle Division who had been left behind by the rest of their unit.

Although it is very difficult to be certain in the various figures discussed about the Soviet losses that occurred in the battle for the city of Bautzen itself, they are estimated at about 1500 soldiers, 4 assault guns and at least 20 T-34/85s. Also, units such as the 7th Mechanized Guard Corps, after the battles for Weissenberg and Bautzen were practically annihilated after suffering losses of 80-90% in both personnel and vehicles. On the other hand, German losses, although equally complicated to establish, were evidently much lower than those of the Soviets.

▲ Close-up of a T-34/85 with the "Orzel Bialy" or white eagle identifying it as belonging to Polish troops. The Polish 2nd Army had more than 200 tanks, including the T-34/85 and the IS-2. Public Domain by Radomil.

► Dresden after the end of World War II was largely destroyed and this photograph is a good example of the state of destruction of the Saxon capital. Public Domain by Deutsche Fotothek.

▼ Although this photograph is taken in Italy during the fighting for Neptune, it serves to show several Sturmgeschütz IIIs and Panthers belonging to the 1st Armored Parachute Division "Hermann Göring". Bundesarchiv.

After the withdrawal of the 2nd Polish Armored Brigade, the 929th Rifle Regiment was left in charge of maintaining the defense in the Rattwitz area. In front of them was the 2nd Battalion of the 1st Regiment of the 1st Armored Parachute Division "Hermann Göring", which after a day of heavy fighting managed to repel the Poles. From there, the men of the 2nd Battalion of the 1st Regiment of the 1st Armored Parachute Division "Hermann Göring" advanced northward, defeating the survivors of the 24th and 26th Guards Mechanized Brigade who were still trying to rebuild their defensive line at Teichnitz.

Farther north of Bautzen, the bulk of the Polish 2nd Army, now under the direct command of Soviet General Vladimir Kostylev, was called in to cover the retreat of the 7th Guards Mechanized Corps that was marching north to meet the 14th and 95th Guards Rifle Divisions and the 4th Guards Armored Corps that were on their way to meet them. Despite many setbacks, the men of the Polish 7th Division along with the Polish 10th Division, which had been completely cut off from the rest of the Polish Army, were ordered to advance on Sdier-Heideanger, and although progress was slow due to German resistance, the 10th Division finally reached the town of Spreefurt and finally secured the road to Königswartha (the Polish unit advanced with its northern flank protected by Soviet units securing the northern part of the road). The Poles managed to rebuild a precarious defensive line (in the eastern part of the front) that frustrated any German possibility of attacking the southern flank of Koniev's troops under siege of Berlin. The defensive line ran through the towns of Kamenz - Kuckau - north of Bautzen - bank of the Spree - Spreewise - Heideanger, and could no longer be "broken" by the Germans.

Recognizing the weakness of the Polish 2nd Army around 13:00 on 25 April, the 1st Parachute Armored Division "Hermann Göring" attacked northwest toward Teichnitz and Kleinwelka. The Panther tanks of the Panzer Regiment "Hermann Göring" under the command of Oberstleutnant Rossman were supported by the men of the 2nd "Hermann Göring" Regiment and the 112th Panzer Grenadier Regiment belonging to the 20th Panzer Division. In reserve were the armored units belonging to the 300th Tank Brigade. The German attack gave its fruits inflicting a hard blow to their opponents, who despite the losses had no intention to surrender, so at 15:00 a Russian attack had to be repulsed with the help of the assault cannons after which the Soviets and the Poles unexpectedly retreated northward. Finally, the Germans were able to continue their advance, taking the villages of Radibor and Grossdubrau with the help of the 21st Panzer Division that had just arrived in that area of the front from its positions further to the northeast and the men of the "Brandenburg" Division that had been redeployed to the front after its action at Weissenberg.

In addition to the 1st Armored Parachute Division "Hermann Göring" (which remained on the left flank of the German attack) with the Withersheim Combat Group, they were also supported by the men of the Panzer-Grenadier Division "Brandenburg" north of Bautzen and on the right flank by the bulk of the 20th Panzer Division (although without its armor).

Once the situation on the front began to stabilize, the Poles also allowed themselves to make small counterattacks that only ended up allowing the Germans to recover between 3 and 5 kilometers.

This was the day when the Soviet air force, completely immersed in the fighting for the capture of Berlin, looked south and immediately regained control of the Saxon skies, which had been largely abandoned during the previous days, allowing Rudel's Stukas to support their comrades on the ground with numerous attacks against enemy armored vehicles and against the pockets of resistance where many of them had been trapped after the retreat from Bautzen.

Although it was evident that the situation was changing in the fighting between the Poles and the Germans, most likely with the intention of boosting the morale of the German units as much as possible, Field Marshal Schörner received congratulations from Adolf Hitler on his important victory in Saxony.

DAY 26. WEDNESDAY

The next day, April 26, there was a heavy engagement near Kleinwelka between Panther tanks of the Panzer Regiment of the 1st Parachute Armored Division "Hermann Göring" and tanks of the Polish 1st Armored Corps. The ferocity of the German thrust again brought down the Poles heavily, giving the impression that enemy resistance was finally broken.

On the left wing of Armoured Parachute Division 1 "Hermann Göring" was the Panzer-Grenadier Division "Brandenburg", which still managed to advance in its attack. The "Brandenburg" with the support of the Panzergruppe Wietersheim, the Assault Corps and the Light Infantry took the village of Loga, as well as the villages of Pannewitz and Krienitz. In Luga a fierce house-to-house fight took place for about half an hour, until the Polish troops retreated. There the men of the "Brandenburg" took 600 prisoners. At the same time to the west, near Panschwitz, the 9th Polish Infantry Division was surrounded and destroyed in its attempt to return to Soviet-occupied territory. Despite these successes, the units of the 4th Panzer Army had failed to achieve their objective: the complete destruction of the Polish 2nd Army and the remnants of the 7th Mechanized Guard Corps, because their attempts to close them in had failed. As the German advance continued, their units had to start repelling attacks by enemy armored troops consisting mainly of T-34s and the powerful Josif Stalin 2.

The German offensive was gradually losing its forward speed due to the increasing resistance offered by the Soviet-Polish. Koniev was determined to prevent further German advances across the Spremberg-Görlitz line, and he decided to take action. On the one hand, he ordered all of his units to prepare anti-tank positions, to create anti-tank force points, and to lay minefields along the German advance routes. It was also necessary to increase the number of troops to face the Germans, so in the end the 9th Polish Division, which was deployed near Dresden, was also called in. This unit, retracing its steps (it was in Bischofwerda), found that the only possible ways to reach the bulk of its troops in the north were through German controlled territory. This order of withdrawal of the 9th Division led by General Aleksander Laski (with little ammunition and without any armored support), meant that the unit suffered numerous losses while crossing areas where many German troops were still deployed, among which were those of the Panzer-Grenadier Division 2 "Hermann Göring" (which since its arrival in Saxony shortly before had been charged with maintaining a defensive line to the west and southwest of Dresden blocking access to the city) as the Poles assumed that the line of retreat was safe; a fact that turned out to be completely wrong. The Germans acted with the advantage of having captured emissaries with orders given to the men of the 9th Division indicating escape routes.

The 9th Division's disaster was of greater proportions at the hands of the 2nd Parachute Panzer-Grenadier Division "Hermann Göring" (although troops from the 1st Parachute Armored Division "Hermann Göring", the Panzer-Grenadier Division "Brandenburg" and Combat Group Wietersheim participated), Thus its 26th Infantry Regiment had up to 75% losses in its attempt to break through the German lines in the area of Panschwitz-Kuckau and Crostwitz where they were ambushed in what was later called by the Poles the "valley of death" (in this ambush Combat Group Wietersheim played an important role). The total losses of the 9th Polish Infantry Division amounted to 4,000 men, all their artillery and all their vehicles; it was a merciless battle. A medical convoy of the 9th Division was also ambushed near Horka. Most of the members of this convoy, about 300 men, were killed and some were captured (such as the head of the unit, Colonel Aleksander Laski) in this attack, there was only one survivor who escaped captivity: Chaplain Jan Rdzanek. As a result of this ordered withdrawal to the 9th Division, one can only think that once again a wrong analysis of the situation by the Polish commanders ended in a new disaster that caused the substantial termination of the 9th Division as an effective combat unit. In fact, the survivors were assigned to a nominally Soviet unit such as the 19th Guards Rifle Division.

All Soviet and Polish units in the area except the 5th Infantry Division (which had remained as a reserve in the Holschka area) prepared to defend their positions at all costs: the 1st Armored Corps, the 7th, 8th, and 10th Polish Infantry Divisions, and Soviet units such as the 5th Guards Army, the 14th, 78th, and 95th Guards Fusilier Divisions, the 150th Armored Brigade, the 4th Guards Armored Corps, the 7th Guards Mechanized Corps, or the 48th Guards Fusilier Corps.

After the destruction of the 9th Polish Infantry Division at Panschwitz-Kuckau and Crostwitz by the 2nd Parachute Panzer-Grenadier Division "Hermann Göring", the Battle of Bautzen was considered over. While it is true that the German offensive in which the town of Bautzen and the surrounding territories were recaptured had indeed ended on 26 April, it is also true that the men of the 1st Parachute Armored Division "Hermann Göring", the Panzer-Grenadier Division "Brandenburg", the 20th Panzer Div, the Withersheim Combat Group and the 21st Panzer Division until April 27th or even 28th continued their advance very slowly until they were completely stopped by the Soviet-Polish (the main weight was carried by the 4th Armored Guard Corps) who established a defensive line in the area between Kamenz and Dauban that would not be crossed by the Germans anymore despite their attacks, which were becoming weaker and weaker (the last German success consisted in the recapture of Kamenz by the Wiethersheim Combat Group).

In spite of this, we cannot forget that sporadic fighting continued until the 30th of the same month with small German groupings that had remained isolated in Soviet territory.

▲ A German Jagdpanzer IV 70 (V) burns while probably being watched by its "hunter," a Red Army T-34/85 tank. This photo was taken in Hungary in March 1945 and gives a very similar picture of what would happen the next month in Lusatia.

▼ Band worn by the troops of the Volksturm (literally People's Strike Force), which was created on October 18, 1944 and composed of males between the ages of 16 and 60 who were not already enlisted in the army.

END OF THE GERMAN OFFENSIVE AND RETREAT

DAY 27. THURSDAY

In the Bautzen area, after the German responses to the Soviet-Polish attacks, the front line remained more or less along the Holschka-Longe axis. Although the German troops had gained a few kilometers, the increased resistance of the Red Army troops was more and more evident with each passing hour. Between April 26 and 27, Soviet resistance became much more intense in the area of Neschwitz, 11 kilometers northwest of Bautzen, as they were reinforced by the 4th Armored Guard Corps of the 2nd Polish Army, which managed to establish a formidable anti-tank barrier there. The 1st Parachute Armored Division "Hermann Göring", the Panzergranader Division "Brandenburg" and the 20th Panzer Division were unable to break through this defensive line due to their impressive anti-tank capabilities. Neschwitz also saw a great deal of fighting in the struggle for the castle and nearby land, which changed hands several times. On April 27, the attack by the 1st Parachute Armored Division "Hermann Göring" finally failed in a wooded area near Holschdubrau east of Neschwitz. Meanwhile, west of Neschwitz the Panzergranader Division "Brandenburg" attempted to capture the town of Casslau which is defended by a large Russian force, but the attack eventually had to be stopped due to the high number of casualties.

DAY 28. FRIDAY

It was not until the morning of the 28th that German troops were finally able to take the town of Casslau after an intense artillery attack and a combined attack by the 20th Panzer Division from the direction of Nausslitz with the support of Hummel and Wespe (self-propelled artillery) vehicles. But despite the new German victory, even there the attack finally had to be stopped and the German units moved into defensive positions due to their inability to continue the attack against an increasingly powerful and well-equipped enemy in the northern direction.

Overall, the German attack was over, reestablishing a defensive line several kilometers above the Rothenburg-Weissenberg-Bautzen line that remained within the German lines. The General Staff of the "Brandenburg" was located east of Dresden, to its right was the 1 Parachute Armored Division "Hermann Göring" (although from 29 it was deployed further west). Continuing the newly established defensive line was the 545th Combat Group of the Volksgrenadier Division, the 464th Division, the 17th Infantry Division and the 72nd Infantry Division along the Spreefurt-Klitten-Neudorf axis. To the left of the General Staff "Brandenburg" were deployed the Combat Group Wiethersheim (in the area of Kamenz after its recapture) and the 2nd Parachute Panzer-Grenadier Division "Hermann Göring" (which held its positions between Kamenz and Dresden) as well as the small Combat Group "Frunsberg" (which remained deployed north of Dresden).

FOLLOWING DAYS

Also during the course of the 29th, German troops attempted to make progress, though with very little confidence in achieving their goal due to the impenetrable defense of Polish and Soviet troops. On the 29th, the 2nd Armored Assault Fighter Regiment of the "Brandenburg" left for Dresden and then moved to Czechoslovakia, where it would continue until the final moments of the world conflict. With the last movements of troops belonging to the 4th Panzer Army, the Panzer-Grenadier Division "Brandenburg" was replaced in the defensive line by the 269th Infantry Division, while the 2nd Parachute Panzer-Grenadier Division "Hermann Göring" was replaced by the 20th Panzer Division.

As mentioned above, on the 30th, once all danger from German units in Saxony was considered over-

▲ A Polish T-34 prepares to cross one of the rivers that will allow it access to German territory by barge. The Poles did not expect the fighting in Lusatia (eastern Saxony) to turn out to be a major setback. By Bpk.Berlin. Benno Wundshammer.

▼ Although this famous photograph shows Hitler Youth in Lauban (Silesia) in March 1945, it is little different from those who had to fight against the Poles and Soviets in the Battle of Bautzen.

come, the Polish 2nd Army and the Soviet forces supporting it, having formed a completely stable defensive line parallel to the one created by the Germans further south between Kamenz-Doberschütz-Dauban, began to prepare for their new objective: the capture of Prague.

On the same day, April 30, the 1st Armored Parachute Division "Hermann Göring" was withdrawn from the front line and moved to Auerbaus, north of Dresden. The front line from 1 May remained without movement on either side until the end of the war as follows: Berinsdorf-Bilea-Zschornau-Schmerlitz-Hoschka-Luppa-Krosta-Tauer-Forstgen-Steinelsa-Kolm-Jekendorf-Serichen-Gross Krauscha-Sodel-Penzig.

On May 1, the remnants of the "Brandenburg" division retreated to the Erz Mountains to occupy defensive positions there, as well as at Olmütz. It was in these areas that the men of the division heard on the radio on 8 May that the Reich had surrendered unconditionally.

After a few last unsuccessful attempts at attacks in the direction of Berlin between 3 and 6 May, the remnants of the "Hermann Göring" marched in columns with numerous civilian refugees mixed in them southwards towards the Erz mountains as early as 7 May. On 8 May 1945, south of Glashütte, on the peaks of the Erz mountains near Geising, the 1st Parachute Armoured Division "Hermann Göring" received news of the German surrender via radio, thus ending the history of the division.

For its part, the 20th Panzer Division after the fighting for Bautzen was deployed northeast of Dresden around April 26, from where then various units of the Division retreated south to Czechoslovakian territory, where on May 6 a part of them surrendered to Red Army troops in the vicinity of Teplice-Sanov; although the rest of the Division managed to surrender to the Americans at Rokycany, between Pilzen and Prague, but they were immediately handed over to the Soviets.

One of the soldiers who distinguished himself in the fighting for Bautzen was Oberstleutnant Rossmann in command of his Armored Regiment of Armored Parachute Division 1 "Hermann Göring," which eventually ended the war by surrendering to American troops in May 1945.

Finally, we recall the fate of one of the protagonists of the battle of Bautzen by the Germans: Dietrich Hoepke; the head of the garrison of Bautzen, who had resisted until the liberation of the city, committed suicide in Reichsstadt (Bohemia) when he heard the news of the capitulation of Germany.

▲ In this magnificent photograph we can appreciate the height of Ortenburg Castle in relation to the old part of the city. Its privileged and isolated location favored its persistence as a center of German resistance until its liberation by the troops of the Hermann Göring", "Brandenburg" and the 20th Panzer Division. Public domain by DB 11 Dörte Bleul.

▲ A pair of Soviet T-34/85s walk the streets of Dresden after its capture at the end of the war. Thanks to the German attack in the Bautzen area, Dresden remained in German hands until the end of the world conflict. Public Domain

▼ Clipping from a newspaper of the time called Schlesische Tageszeitung showing containers used to supply troops and the fenced-in population of Breslau.

RESULTS AND CONCLUSIONS

The final success of the German Reich with the capture of Bautzen and Weissenberg resulted in a large number of casualties on both sides, as well as destroyed vehicles and armored vehicles of all types.

It was the Soviet-Polish who bore the heaviest burden in the area between Bautzen and Dresden, due to the heavy losses especially of their Polish units. According to current studies, it is estimated that the Polish 2nd Army suffered about 22% losses in terms of killed and wounded, while in terms of tank and armored vehicle potential, losses exceeded 57% with the destruction of 170 tanks and 56 self-propelled guns. They suffered heavy damage in other aspects as well, such as the loss of 124 mortars, 232 cannons of all types, 330 vehicles and 1373 horses. Polish losses were estimated at 4,902 dead, 10,532 wounded and 2,798 missing: this corresponds to about 27% of the losses of the Polish Army between October 1943 and May 1945 (although this figure of about 18,000 men could be adjusted according to some sources even to about 25,000, which would correspond in this case to about one third of the potential of the Polish 2nd Army before the start of the campaign for Bautzen). For their part, the Soviet units of the 7th Mechanized Guard Corps lost at least 3,500 men, 81 tanks, and 45 self-propelled guns; which corresponded to about 87% of their armored fleet before these fights.

According to a Luftkommando 6 report of 27 April (sources by Stephan Hamilton), the Germans caused the Soviet-Polish enemy between 20 and 26 April in the Bautzen area, at least the destruction of 355 tanks, 329 guns of different calibers, 7,000 dead and about 800 prisoners.

Although also considerable, the losses suffered by the Germans were quantitatively lower. Thus, it is estimated that the various German units of the 4th Panzer Army lost 6,500 men between dead, wounded and missing (remember the difficulty of knowing these figures exactly, so for example more recent studies even reduce this figure). To these must be added about 1,200 dead and missing members of the German garrison in Bautzen and about 350 civilian residents of Bautzen who were involved in the maelstrom of fighting between the two sides for the Polish capture and subsequent German reconquest of the city.

Bautzen was severely damaged after the fighting, with most of its homes destroyed. It is estimated that at least 10% of the homes of the civilian population were completely destroyed, as well as 33% of the storage buildings, 35 public buildings, as well as more than 50 of the various factories in the area and 18 bridges. And what was not destroyed was however severely damaged in the fierce fighting both during the capture by the Poles and during the subsequent reconquest by the Germans, although fortunately many historic buildings still remained standing and have been restored and are in excellent condition today.

From the strategic point of view, the last German victory brought only some benefits to the Reich in its first days of the campaign, since immediately afterwards it was possible to verify the German inability to cut off the communications of the 1st Ukrainian Front and to expel the Poles from the east of Saxony, turning into a possible danger for the adequate employment of the 1st Ukrainian Front against the German capital. Although the high command of the 4th Panzer Army knew of the real inability of its troops to "break" the 1st Ukrainian Front on its southern flank and support the besieged Berlin due to the lack of fuel and ammunition, it managed to keep it under control for a few days and succeeded in getting other Soviet forces sent to the Bautzen region, thus avoiding their participation in the taking of Berlin. In fact, on April 25 at 2:30 p.m., Generaloberst Alfred Jodl requested by radio from the General Staff of Army Group Center that the 4th Armored Army extend its offensive northward to relieve pressure on the Reich's capital; and on the night of April 26-27, Adolf Hitler himself gave the order by telephone to the General Staff of Army Group Center for the same purpose.

Finally, after the German offensive north of Bautzen was stopped due to the strong resistance of the growing Soviet forces and the practical lack of fuel and ammunition on the German side, the Saxon region was occupied by the Soviets, although those few days that managed to remain in German hands, allowed the escape of many civilians and even soldiers to the west to surrender and surrender to the Western Allies, avoiding falling into the hands of the Soviets. Only on May 9, after the German capitulation, the destroyed city of Dresden was captured, when the capital of the Reich had already been captured 6 days before.

The last victory of the German armed forces in World War II is rather controversial depending on who evaluates it, as both sides claimed victory. In fact, the Soviets considered their incursion into Saxony as a strategic triumph and therefore all the events related to the capture of Bautzen were just a few inconveniences that had no significance for the final victory of their strategy of taking the capital of the Reich at any cost. In fact, the war was practically over and the Soviet triumph on the Eastern Front was indisputable.

The Poles, who were among the protagonists of the battles for Bautzen, after the end of the world conflict claimed the actions for Bautzen as a complicated victory, but a victory nonetheless. Evidently, they could not recognize the multiple failures in the command and chain of command of their units and of course the huge number of human and material losses, since Poland was destined under the Soviet mantle behind the "Iron Curtain". Today, many years have passed since the end of the pro-Soviet communist regime in 1991, and historians in Poland have developed a more critical view of the Battle of Bautzen. Thus, the commander-in-chief of the Polish Second Army, General Świerczewski, who after the end of the war was considered a "war hero" and was appointed Marshal of Poland, is no longer regarded so positively today. On the contrary, General Świerczewski today is considered to be primarily responsible for the destruction and loss of a large part of the army under his command due to his numerous tactical errors and inadequate strategy which deviated "significantly" from the orders received from Marshal Koniev, directing his troops quickly to the capture of the city of Dresden. Moreover, it is also pointed out today that the general himself commanded his troops in an obvious state of drunkenness on several occasions, his collaboration with Stalin's purges or the very light training and preparation of a large part of the Polish troops still "immature for combat". As a curiosity, General Świerczewski died in an unclear way in counter-insurgency actions towards Ukrainian guerrillas in 1947 not before being transformed by Stalin's regime into a true genius of strategy for the Polish people. In reality not only the Polish general was questioned, but also other commanders of his Polish 2nd Army who made certain decisions without the proper preparation, as happened to the commander of the 9th Polish Infantry Division which was practically 100% destroyed. In the end, in spite of all this, this campaign from the passage of the Neisse is still generally regarded in Poland as a hard-fought victory in which the German troops eventually had to surrender.

On the other hand, other historians, including German historians, view the events around Bautzen as a magnificent example of a tactical victory, despite the fact that Germany was virtually defeated. In fact, German troops of the 4th Panzer Army were able to recapture Bautzen, Weissenberg, and the surrounding area. This territory that extended towards Dresden remained in German hands until the end of the war, allowing the already mentioned "escape" of thousands of people to the western zone of Allied occupation beyond the Elbe. Let us not forget that these German units, exhausted by years of fighting, and who took part in the battle of Bautzen, together with some other units, would in some cases continue the fight against the Red Army and the Czech insurgents in Czechoslovakia.

Another element to consider during the fighting was the air weapon. The Soviets had a large number of units (thousands) that continuously supported them with numerous sorties against the threatening German troops. For its part, the Luftwaffe could do little because of the undeniable air dominance of the Allies and their chronic lack of fuel. Despite this, they were able to produce hundreds of sorties

▲ Side view of a Polish IS-2, as can be recognized by its white eagle on the turret. Although on paper the Polish 2nd Army was very powerful, it had numerous operational problems due to the poor preparation of its troops.

▼ A T-34/85 of the Soviet 7th Armored Corps is tuned by its crew during the offensive for Prague.

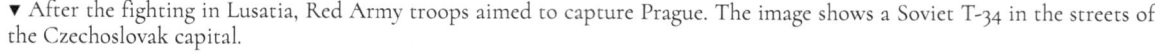

▲ The Panzerjäger battalion of the Panzergrenadier Division "Brandenburg" was equipped with L/48 Jagdpanzer IVs that effectively fulfilled their task as this example displayed in the Panzer Museum in Munster. In the latter stages of the war, tank destroyers and assault guns were often used as replacements for tanks due to the shortage of tanks in German units. Public Domain by Banznerfahrer.

▼ After the fighting in Lusatia, Red Army troops aimed to capture Prague. The image shows a Soviet T-34 in the streets of the Czechoslovak capital.

in support of their comrades on the ground. It was here that Stukas ace Hans Ulrich Rudel with his small unit of Stukas tank destroyers managed to knock out at least 26 tanks (3 of which were joined by Rudel himself).

German historians consider after all that within such an important military operation as that carried out by the Soviets from their positions in the Neisse which in little more than half a month ended with the general German capitulation, the performance of the troops of the 4th Panzer Army succeeded against all expectations in creating a serious crisis in the overall advance of the 1st Ukrainian Front. Even though this crisis did not spread further due to the often mentioned difficulties only a couple of weeks before the end of the war in a completely shattered Germany. The number of Soviet-Polish human and material casualties was significantly higher than that of German troops and the reconquest of territory was maintained until the capitulation, so today there is no longer any doubt, Bautzen was indeed the last German victory in World War II.

▲ Above: a Panther of the 1st Parachute Armored Division "Hermann Göring" destroyed during the fighting in East Prussia in February 1945. In these battles the men of the Luftwaffe's elite unit demonstrated their courage and daring, just as they would do shortly thereafter in the Saxon lands. Top: the other "workhorse" of the 1st Parachute Armored Division "Hermann Göring" was the late-model Panzer IV. Although it was a tank already outclassed by more modern tanks, it served its purpose perfectly until the end of the war. The Pz IV pictured shows its side skirt and winter camouflage used during the fighting in East Prussia in early 1945.

▲ Although we have not found data to fully verify this, it is quite possible that the Jagdpanzer 38 "Hetzer" was also part of the armored and mechanized divisions during the battles described in this book.

▼ Polish T-34/85 with its crew. Thanks to this tank and the IS-2, the reborn Polish armored forces under the auspices of the U.S.S.R. on paper became serious contenders for the Germans. The facts would prove otherwise during the fighting for Bautzen.

▲ Soviet aircraft did not completely dominate the Saxon skies during the Oder-Neisse offensive, because their presence in the Berlin area was intensified and neglected in Saxony. But they inevitably took control of the Saxon skies when the battle for Berlin was all but decided in favor of the Soviets. Pictured is a grouping of the lethal Il-2 attack aircraft in April 1945.

▼ Image of a Junkers Ju 87 G-2 with two 37 mm subalar guns belonging to SG 2 in 1945. These aircraft led by their leader Hans Ulrich Rudel were among the main architects of the German victory over the Soviets and Poles in East Saxony.

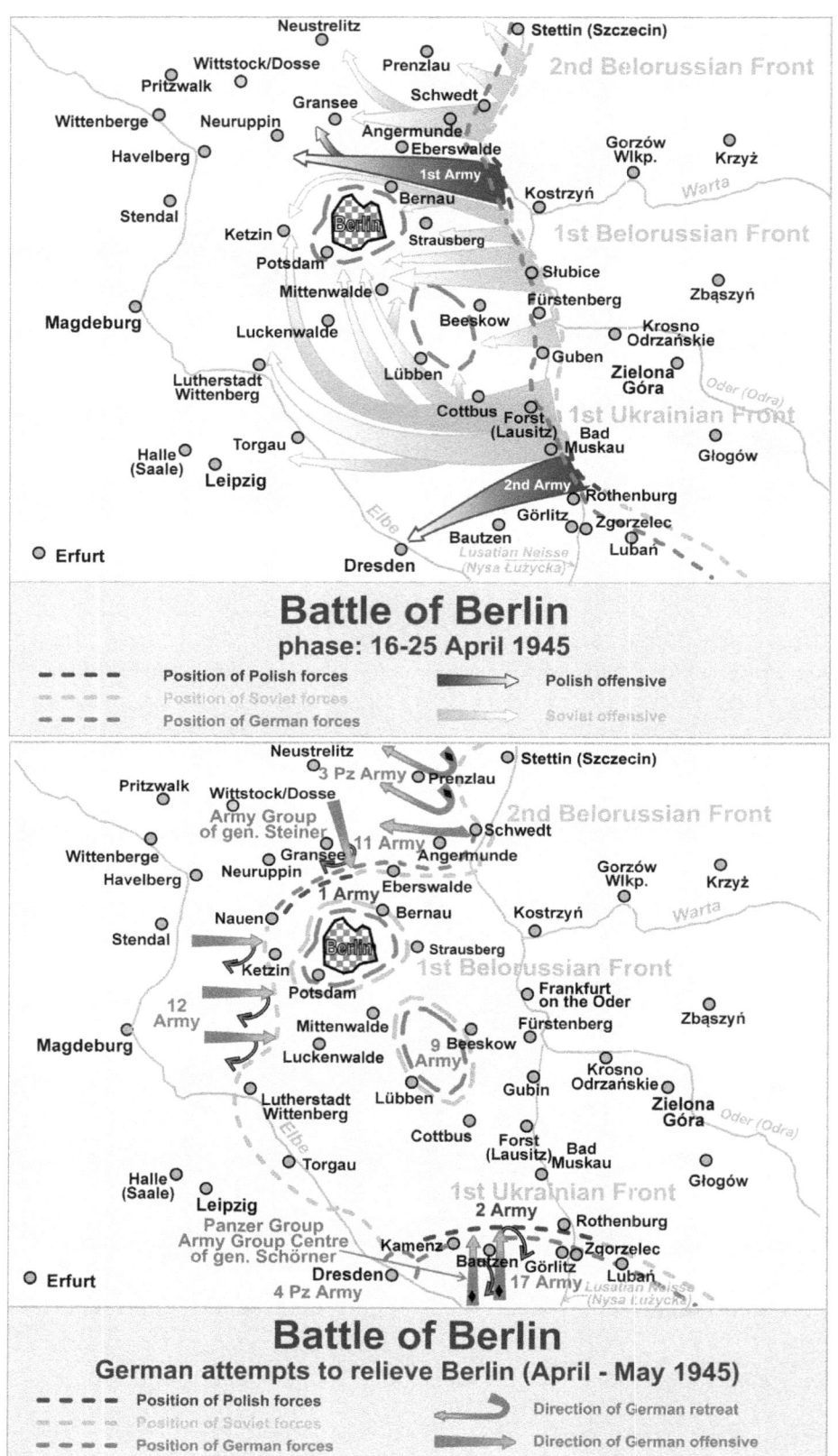

BIBLIOGRAPHY

-Antill, P. *Berlin 1945. End of the thousand year Reich*. Osprey Publishing. 2005.
-Hans von Ahlfen (1977). *Der Kampf um Schlesien 1944/1945*. Stuttgart: Motorbuch Verlag.
-Bahn, Karl. *Berlin 1945. The final reckoning*. MBI publishing company. 2001.
-Beevor, Anthony. *"Berlín. La caída: 1945"*. Crítica S.L 2002.
-Eberhard Berndt (1995). *"Die Kämpfe um Bautzen 18. bis 27. April 1945"*. Lipsia
-Cristini Luca. *Berlin 1945*. Soldiershop 2020
-Duffy, Christopher. *"Red storm on the Reich. The Soviet march on Germany 1945"*. Routledge. 1991.
-Wolfgang Fleischer (2004). *Das Kriegsende in Sachsen 1945*. Dörfler.
-Gil Martínez, Eduardo Manuel. *Breslau 1945*. Soldiershop. 2020.
-Gil Martínez, Eduardo Manuel. *Españoles en las SS y la Wehrmacht. La unidad Ezquerra en la batalla de Berlín 1945*. Almena. 2011.
-Gil Martínez, Eduardo Manuel. *Fuerzas acorazadas húngaras 1939-45*. Almena. 2017.
-Goebbels, Joseph. *"Diario de 1945"*. La esfera de los libros. 2007.
-Czesław Grzelak; *Armia Berlinga i Żymierskiego (Army of Berling and Żymierski)*. Warszawa 2002
-Harrison, Richard W. *The Berlin operation, 1945*. Helion & Company. 2016.
-Heiberg, Heiber. *"Hitler y sus generales"*. Crítica S.L. 2005.
-Hinze, Rolf. *To the bitter end*. Casemate. 2013.
-Holzträger, Hans. *"In a raging inferno. Combat units of the Hitler Youth 1944-45"*. Helion. 2000.
-Jacobsen, HA. Dollinger, H. *La Segunda Guerra Mundial*. Plaza & Janés Editores S.A. 1989.
-Lopez, Jean. *Berlin, les offensives géantes de l'Armée rouge: vistule-Oder-Elbe*. 2011
-Kurowski, F. *Hitler's last bastion. The final battles for the Reich. 1944-1945*. Schiffer Military History. 1998.
-Mahé, Yann. *Carnage à Bautzen*. Hors Series Batailles& Blindes nº 51. 2012.
-Mitcham, Samuel W. *"German order of battle. Volume one"*. Stackpole Books. 2007.
-Mitcham, Samuel W. *"German order of battle. Volume two"*. Stackpole Books. 2007.
-Oliver, Dennis. *Panther tanks*. Pen & Sword. 2019.
-Oliver, Dennis. *To the last bullet*. The Oliver publishing group. 2010.
-Ryan, C. *La última batalla. La caída de Berlín y la derrota del nazismo*. Salvat.2003.
-Simons, G. *La Segunda Guerra Mundial. Victoria en Europa* I.Time Life Folio.1995.
-Stephan Hamilton, A. *Panzergrenadiers to the front*. Helion. 2016.
-Williamson, G.; Andrew, Stephen. *The Hermann Göring Division*. Osprey. 2003.
-Tirone, Laurent. *Panzer. The German tanks encyclopedia*. Caraktere. 2016.
-Urbanke, Axel.*Endkampf um das Reichsgebiet 1944-1945-*. Luftfahrverlag START. 2009.
-Zaloga, Steven J. *Downfall 1945*. Osprey Publishing 2016.
-Ziemke, Earl F. *"La batalla de Berlín fin del Tercer Reich"*. San Martín 1982.
-Axis History Forum.

TITLES ALREADY PUBLISHING

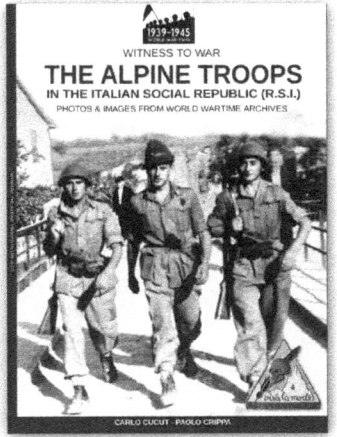
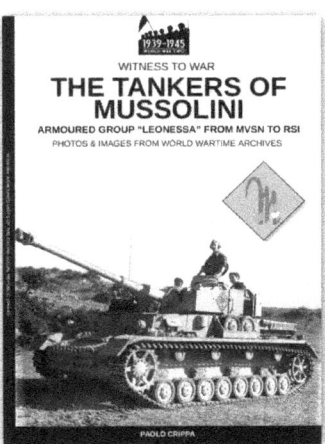

www.ingramcontent.com/pod-product-compliance
Ingram Content Group UK Ltd.
Pitfield, Milton Keynes, MK11 3LW, UK
UKHW050411240426
12048UKWH00020B/1461